BUILDING A NEW CHURCH ALONGSIDE THE OLD

Also by Martin Down:

Building a
New Church
Alongside the Old

MARTIN DOWN

KINGSWAY PUBLICATIONS
EASTBOURNE

ISBN 1 84291 139 2

Published by
KINGSWAY COMMUNICATIONS LTD
Lottbridge Drove, Eastbourne BN23 6NT, England.
Email: books@kingsway.co.uk

Book design and production for the publishers by
Bookprint Creative Services, P.O. Box 827, BN21 3YJ, England.
Printed in Great Britain.

Contents

Acknowledgements

I would like to thank the following people for their help with specific sections of this book. They have been kind enough to give me their time and to check the accuracy of the information. That does not mean, of course, that they can be held responsible for the views that I express in this book, which are my own. I am aware also that at many more points I am indebted to books I have read and people I have talked to over a lifetime. If someone recognises an idea or a phrase of their own which is unattributed, it is only because I have forgotten where I first heard or saw it.

I thank William Sayer for help with the section on Wells-next-the-Sea; Alan Dodds on the Carpenter's Arms, Deal; Ove Conrad Hanssen, Martin Cave and others on Imi Kirken, Stavanger; Annie Gauthier-Vandroux and members of the Community of the Beatitudes, Cuisery, on new communities in France; Mike Clarkson on Oak Tree Anglican Fellowship, Acton; Graham Hall on Norwich Community Church; and Nicky Gumbel on the history of the Alpha course at Holy Trinity, Brompton.

Foreword

It is common knowledge that church attendance has declined hugely in recent decades. It is also true that the Christian story no longer lies at the heart of British society or self-consciousness. Religion is seen by many as a leisure pursuit competing with many other leisure pursuits. It is for those who 'like that sort of thing'.

For many, church seems more a memorial to a bygone age than a relevant option today, and some churches are only seen as important heritage sites. We live between the times in an era when traditional church is still deeply meaningful for some and perfectly capable of reaching out imaginatively, but there are perhaps as many for whom the cultural barrier is simply too high. We need both traditional church and new forms of church. We need them alongside each other, in partnership and in a thought-out strategy. We need both/and, not either/or.

That is why this book is so important and so timely. I have known Martin Down for a long time, and know first hand much of the story which underlies his book. It has been a very blessed and a very painful journey, which now has a highly satisfactory outcome. There are many lessons here for the whole church to learn. There are lessons that can help other churches take new initiatives, and lessons that can help them avoid unnecessary pain.

The church is missionary to its core. Mission is of its essence, for it is called to share in God's mission, through Christ, by the Spirit. The eternal gospel we have received may not be changed if we are to remain true to our Christian inheritance. Jesus our Lord is as attractive and compelling as ever. But the cultural form of the church must be open to change, if it is to be true to its calling to proclaim the good news of Christ afresh in each generation. Both mission fields – the culturally traditional and the culturally new – are ripe and ready. We need new church alongside the old in town and country.

I strongly commend this book to all those who are concerned about the future mission of Christ's church, whether they share Martin's tradition within it, or belong to another.

Graham Cray
Bishop of Maidstone

Introduction

Most people recognise that the long-drawn-out decline of the English churches in the twentieth century, and of the Church of England in particular, is now approaching some sort of crisis. The shape of the Church of England in ten years' time is likely to be radically different. We need a new vision of the church, of its relationship to society and the world around it, of its calling to the world, and of structures that will enable that vision to be fulfilled and that calling to be served.

This book may not tell people what they want to hear, whether they are bishops, clergy, or those few people still sitting in the pews of our country churches. People want to be told that all is well, that everyone is doing a wonderful job in very difficult circumstances, that heart-warming things are happening all around, and that just hanging on in there will see us through. But I doubt this. We have gone on doing the same old things in the same old way with the same old results for too long now for me to have any confidence that it is only a matter of time before they start working again. I think we have to look much deeper, to discover the reasons for the parlous position we are in and the remedies we need. I am offering in this book an analysis rather than a blueprint, but in the process I think we can find some useful pointers to the way forward. I have come to the conclusion that this way forward involves radical

11

changes in the structures of the Church of England, more radical than many may be willing to accept, but changes which I believe can be seen and embraced positively rather than accepted reluctantly and grudgingly.

This book is not mere theory. It is the result of more than 30 years' experience of rural ministry in the Church of England; ministry which has included the classical pattern of one parish, one priest, and the modern pattern of the multi-parish benefice; ministry exercised as a stipendiary minister working on his own, and at another time working with a team of nonstipendiary ministers and lay readers; ministry ranging from traditional Anglican, consciously modelled on George Herbert's *Country Parson*, to charismatic, modelled more on John Wimber, founder of Vineyard Ministries. This is the voice of one who has worked through all the panaceas and fashions of late-twentieth-century Anglican ministry: liturgical reform, ecumenism, collaborative styles of ministry, pastoral reorganisation, and a variety of attempts at mission and evangelism. It is the voice of one who now finds himself outside the traditional structures of the Church of England altogether, leading a new church, sometimes now called a 'network church', still in the heart of the countryside and still in the Church of England, but only just. Against the background of the traditional structures of the church, our present position is precarious and anomalous. Nonetheless, I believe that our new church, and others like it, may be a sign of the new church that is to come.

I wrote two books in the 1990s, *Speak to These Bones* and *Streams of Living Water*, describing my experience of leading two traditional country churches, St Nicholas's and St George's, into renewal. It was a painful and sad experience as well as a joyful and exciting one. In some ways this book is the third instalment of what has come to resemble a real-life soap-opera, a sort of charismatic *Archers*. Those who have read the previous books will find here less story and more analysis. I hope that those who have not read the previous volumes will not find themselves at too great a disadvantage.

PART ONE

Three Stages of Renewal

1

Personal Renewal

By 'renewal' I mean specifically the renewal of the work and the manifestations of the Holy Spirit in the lives of Christian believers and in the life of the church. Like all works of grace, this renewal is the product of a mysterious interaction between the sovereign will of God and the desires and longings of the human heart.

I believe that, above everything else, the twentieth century will go down in church history as the century of the Holy Spirit. The beginning of the Pentecostal movement is dated to 1906 at the Azusa Street Mission in Los Angeles, California. In one hundred years the churches which trace their origins to that famous revival have become the third force in Christendom, challenging both Catholics and Protestants, and in terms of numerical growth outstripping us all. This twentieth-century outpouring of the Holy Spirit has been likened to Israel's latter rain. The early rain was the initial out-pouring on the day of Pentecost and on the generation of the apostles; the latter rain is this modern re-emergence of the supernatural gifts and power of the Holy Spirit, associated initially with Pentecostalism.

In the second part of the twentieth century the mainline denominations themselves began to open up to the person and work of the Holy Spirit in a new way. This opening up became known as the charismatic movement, or charismatic renewal. David du Plessis, a South African Pentecostal who became a crucial bridge back to the mainline denominations in the middle of the century, recorded a remarkable prophecy given to him in 1937 by Smith Wigglesworth:

> The door of my office in Johannesburg suddenly opened and before me stood Smith Wigglesworth the Pentecostalist from England . . . He began to prophesy and to tell of visions that he had had – a great multitude in great churches all over the world. He said that God was going to bring about a spiritual renewal through the old-line denominations . . . The awakening, he said, would be Pentecostal in nature but would be far more powerful and effective than the Pentecostal Movement outside the churches . . . He said that the revival would not begin in his lifetime but would begin soon after his death . . . He emphasised that the old-line denominations would become the channel through which the Holy Spirit would work. It would be as it was in the beginning when (Acts 6:7) 'the number of disciples multiplied and increased greatly and a great company of the priests were obedient to the faith'. Contrary to what we had seen in the 20th century up to that time the new movement would begin primarily as a renewal amongst the clergy.

Every day, I give thanks and praise to God that on the 29th June 1983 I became one of those priests in the 'old-line' denominations who came into this wonderful renewal, and I want nothing more than that all my clerical brothers and sisters and the congregations committed to their charge should also come into this glorious new life in the Holy Spirit of Jesus.

My experience of leading two traditional country churches into renewal, and my study of the experiences of others, has led me to believe that renewal proceeds in three stages:

Stage 1: the renewal of the individual
Stage 2: the renewal of the congregation
Stage 3: the renewal of the structures

Renewal can break down at any one of these stages, and it will break down if the individuals and especially the leaders concerned are not prepared to push through the barriers at each stage – for there are indeed barriers and opposition at every stage. Equally, there is no way by which any stage of progress can be omitted. Each phase, if it is not to be mere cosmetic change, depends on the previous one. There are no short cuts. There is no spiritual renewal of the congregation without the spiritual renewal of the individuals in that congregation. In turn, there is no meaningful renewal of the structures of the church without the spiritual renewal of congregations.

There are all sorts of substitutes and deceptions which masquerade as renewal. The renewal of the individual is not just a matter of old Christian dogs learning new Christian tricks. The renewal of the congregation is not just introducing a worship band and singing some new songs. The renewal of the structures is not just a scheme to reorder the medieval church or change a few boundaries on the map. Renewal is not the same thing as modernisation. Most traditional churches have taken steps towards modernisation; far fewer have taken steps towards renewal in the Holy Spirit.

The first step is the renewal of individuals, and the first individual in the church who needs to be renewed is the leader. I believe that the correct scriptural term for this renewal is 'the baptism of the Holy Spirit'. Others prefer to speak about being filled with the Holy Spirit or about the release of the Holy Spirit. My own theology of this concept is contained in the appendix on pages 184–188. I am not prepared, however, to argue for my own theology over anybody else's. People may hold a different theology or use a different terminology and still end up in the same spiritual place: born again and filled with the Holy Spirit. The basic necessity for the baptism of the Holy Spirit is a sense of need, the need of God's power, and a radical openness to whatever God has to give or wants to do. Such radical openness is simply expressed in the prayer 'Come, Holy Spirit', without any ifs or buts.

The ifs or buts we are tempted to add are legion. There are the trivial ones: 'but I won't fall down'; 'but I don't want to speak in tongues'; 'but I shan't lose control of my emotions'. In his mercy and grace, God often seems to answer our prayers in spite of our qualifications, and deals with those later. There are more serious provisos, however, that put bigger obstacles in the way of God's work: 'Come, Holy Spirit ... provided you don't upset anyone'; '. . . provided you don't change our traditions or habits'; '. . . provided I can still control the agenda'. The Holy Spirit simply will not come on our private terms, or if he comes he will soon be so grieved that he will depart again before long.

Personal renewal involves a radical change in the interior life, a quantum leap forward in an individual's relationship to God, and a no less radical change in the individual's relationship to others, especially other Spirit-filled Christians in the household of faith. These changes are not self-induced or the result of effort on our own part; they are sovereign works of the Holy Spirit entering into and filling our hearts and minds.

Being Spirit-filled does not mean being perfect. If we are Spirit-filled and we say we have no sin, we still deceive ourselves and the truth is not in us (1 John 1:8). Being Spirit-filled means that we no longer have to depend on our brothers and sisters to teach us to know the Lord, because each one of us, from the least to the greatest, knows the Lord for him- or herself (Jeremiah 31:31–34). It means that we can learn to hear the voice behind us, which is the voice of the Holy Spirit, saying, 'This is the way; walk in it' (Isaiah 30:21). It means that we have received both a new spirit and a new heart, so that we not only feel obliged to keep God's commandments, but want to do so (Ezekiel 36:26–27). It remains possible at every moment for us to resist, quench or grieve the Holy Spirit, but as we learn to respond to and walk by the Spirit, so the character of Jesus is formed in us, the fruit of love, joy, peace, patience, kindness, goodness, faithfulness, gentleness and self-control (Galatians 5:22–23).

Being filled with the Holy Spirit also means that we can expect to receive and move in the supernatural gifts of the Spirit: the revelation gifts of wisdom, knowledge, prophecy and discernment, the prayer gifts of faith and tongues, and the practical gifts of miracles and healing (1 Corinthians 12:8–10). It is because this renewal has produced fresh manifestations of these supernatural gifts (or *charismata* in Greek) that it has rightly been called the charismatic renewal.

To be filled with the Holy Spirit is also to discover or develop gifts of ministering to or serving others that we did not have or did not use before: gifts of evangelism in leading other people to faith in Jesus Christ, gifts of pastoral care, practical help and administration, gifts of teaching adults, children or young people, and artistic gifts of music, design or writing.

Perhaps, above all, being filled with the Holy Spirit is to discover in ourselves a new capacity to love God with all our heart, mind, soul and strength, to express that love in worship and adoration, and to discover in ourselves a new capacity to love our neighbours in warm and affectionate ways.

To bring people into life in the Spirit, it is necessary before all else to teach them – about Jesus and about the Holy Spirit. People need to be brought one by one to the place where they believe in Jesus as Lord and Saviour and are open to receive the baptism of the Holy Spirit. There are many ways of doing this, formally or informally, but I know no better way than the Alpha course. It seems to me that no church can do without some mechanism for bringing new people (as well as the existing congregation if necessary) into saving faith in Jesus and the fullness of the Holy Spirit as an ongoing part of its normal life. There is no better recommendation for the Alpha course than that it works: it does these jobs in a way that is accessible and acceptable to the people of our generation. But in the end, these things are accomplished by the simplest of prayers: the sinner's prayer and the invocation of the Holy Spirit, prayers said as expressions of a heart's desire, a desire for forgiveness and for the power of God; prayers said not as a single event, but prayers which become attitudes for the whole of the rest of our lives.

* * *

Maureen's story is in many ways typical of someone of her generation. As a child she attended both a Church of England primary and a Church of England secondary school in rural Berkshire. At an appropriate age she was encouraged by the vicar, who came into the school, to be confirmed. Many of her friends were being confirmed, so Maureen went along too. At no time did anyone mention either the possibility or the necessity of a personal commitment to Jesus Christ.

One person stood out for Maureen in her schooldays: the headmistress of the secondary school seemed to possess an indefinable 'something', which Maureen later came to realise was a personal faith. After she left school, however, even these tenuous links with the church and Christianity were broken, and Maureen drifted into a godless and worldly way of life. It was some years later, while working as a secretary in London, that she next came across that indefinable 'something' she had seen in her old headmistress. She found the same quality in a man who became her boss. His integrity and consideration for others, in a large international organisation, stood out. Although he never preached sermons to his staff, his conversation and attitudes revealed his profound personal faith. Under his influence Maureen started going to church again, and gravitated to All Saints, Margaret Street, a well-known Anglo-Catholic church in the heart of London. Since the village church in Berkshire where Maureen had grown up was also of this tradition, she assumed that this was just what church was like.

At All Saints, Maureen learned the truth about God and about the sacrifice of Christ; she discovered the love and care of other Christians, not least the priests on the staff. Here she did learn that a personal commitment to Christ was necessary, and one day, while walking in Hyde Park near Marble Arch, she made her commitment to him.

However, she still found a sense of remoteness and unreality about her Christian experience. Through all the bells and smells, the rites and ceremonies of Anglo-Catholic worship, she was still conducting a desperate search for something more.

Soon after this, Maureen married a young Anglican curate and together they moved to the strange climate of the north of England. The years that followed, first in industrial northern towns and then in country villages, were full of the business of making homes, raising children and being the vicar's wife. Spiritually, however, they were years of wandering in the wilderness of 'middle-of-the-road' Anglicanism which left her feeling even further away from God. As to reaching others with the faith, how could she tell others about a God who was scarcely real to her?

One day, a mobile library of Christian books called the Good News Van turned up in her village. Although at first she could not be persuaded to borrow any books, this little van was to be the means by which Maureen found what she had been seeking for so long and which was to turn her life round completely and for ever. Through the Good News Van she and her husband were invited to hear an Anglican bishop speak at a nearby town about his experience of the Holy Spirit. The bishop was highly entertaining, amusing and witty, and he spoke about how he, already a bishop, had come into the baptism of the Holy Spirit. There was no heavy theology, just an invitation to receive anything that was going from God. Maureen had not even realised that anything *might* be going from God, and found bells starting to ring inside. Was God actually going to give her something? As the bishop prayed at the end, Maureen was open to everything God had to give.

Nothing dramatic happened at the time, but soon afterwards other people began to notice a difference in her; even her daughter, then aged 15, remarked that Mum was happier. Indeed, Maureen, without being fully aware of it, had never been truly happy for as long as she could remember, but now she found springing up inside her a little fountain of joy which had never been there before and which, despite many hardships and difficulties, has never gone away.

Maureen began to talk to others about Jesus, and found that her earlier embarrassment about mentioning his name had mysteriously disappeared. She gave her testimony at a church meeting, went door to door visiting as part of a parish mission, and joined the team of the Good News Van, now devouring the books about life in the Spirit herself, as well as recommending them to others.

Many fresh fillings and touches of the Holy Spirit followed, not least through the Christian family conference called New Wine and a visit in 1995 to the Airport Vineyard in Toronto. Back in the parish, Maureen was now involved in the life and ministry of the church as never before, constantly growing in understanding, and in the boldness to tell others the good news and give away what she herself had so desperately sought for so long.

*   *   *

Maureen, whose story I have just told, is my own wife, whom I have known intimately for 35 years. If I ever need to be assured that the baptism of the Holy Spirit is real, I have only to look at her, and see the wonderful thing that God has done in her life.

2

Congregational Renewal

Renewal at the level of the individual Christian believer has progressed a long way in the last 40 years. Alongside the growth of Pentecostalism, which has been steady if not spectacular in Britain, the result of the charismatic renewal in the mainline churches means that Spirit-filled Christians are to be found today in every town and village in the land. The river of God is ankle deep everywhere. But by no means all these Spirit-filled Christians are to be found in Pentecostal or charismatic churches. At the level of the congregation, the progress of renewal has been much slower.

It is not difficult to find Spirit-filled Christians who are frustrated at being in churches in which the leaders do not want to know about the things of the Spirit. Equally, it is not difficult to find Spirit-filled church leaders who are frustrated at being in churches in which the people are stuck fast in the old traditional ways. Such mismatches are commonplace. There is, however, an even more curious situation, which is not unusual either: both the leader and many of the people want to move on in the Spirit, and yet nothing in the church changes. The renewal of the congregation is a different matter from the renewal of the individual.

A renewed church is one in which the person and work of the Holy Spirit are given due place. The place due to the Holy

Spirit is a place equal to that of the Father and the Son, because in the Trinity, as the Athanasian Creed puts it, 'the whole three Persons are co-eternal and co-equal'. In many churches, even Jesus the Son struggles to get equal recognition with God the Father. Many an evangelical vicar has been chastised because he keeps on preaching about Jesus. But in many churches the Holy Spirit finds it even harder to establish a place. The Holy Spirit is indeed for many 'the third man', as in Graham Greene's book, a shadowy figure whose very existence is uncertain.

In a renewed church, the Holy Spirit is openly honoured and welcomed. There is freedom during the gatherings of the church for the Holy Spirit to move, and for his supernatural gifts to be imparted and received. When the Holy Spirit comes in power upon individuals or the whole congregation, the manifestations of that power are welcomed and blessed. The worship of a renewed church allows the members to express their love of God with passion and intimacy; there is real interaction between the members of the congregation as well as real interaction with God; there is an atmosphere of freedom and joy. Above all, the congregation is sensitive and obedient to the agenda and purpose of God for his people. They seek to be aware of what God is doing and where he is leading his church today. Many people have experienced such interaction with God and with one another at Christian Bible weeks or conferences; fewer have managed to transfer them successfully into the life of the local church.

There is no way in which a traditional church can be renewed without the active co-operation of the appointed leaders. David Watson used to describe the clergyman as the cork in the bottle. The Holy Spirit cannot get past him, but must go through him if he is to enter the church at all. It is one of the awesome mysteries of the kingdom of God that God respects the leaders of his church and their wishes so much. If a leader says, 'I do not want my church to be known as charismatic,' the Holy Spirit will tiptoe away: he knows when and where he is not wanted.

Spirit-filled Christians in un-Spirit-filled churches under un-Spirit-filled leaders face difficult choices: to stay and pray in all humility for better days to come, or to leave and find a church whose leader they can more wholeheartedly follow. Many have started off determined to stay and pray for change, only to decide some years later that life is too short and the kingdom too urgent for that. The problem is particularly acute when there are children and young people to be considered. For most parents, the prime consideration must be to find a church where their children will be excited about God and will find other young people who will provide a Christian peer group for them as they grow up.

The new churches which have sprung up and been planted all over the land in the last 30 years are the fruit of such frustration: Christians newly filled with the Holy Spirit finding no encouragement and sometimes active discouragement from their local church and vicar have moved out to join or form new churches. God has blessed these new churches, bringing many of them together into new networks – New Frontiers, Pioneer, Vineyard, and other regional groupings. These new churches are the only ones which have grown consistently over the last 30 years, and if they have sometimes grown at the expense of the older denominations, the older denominations have only themselves to blame.

There are two sources of real difficulty in leading a traditional church into renewal. The first is timidity, or at least a misunderstanding of the church's role and calling. The second is the structures of the church.

When a traditional congregation is first exposed to teaching about the person and work of the Holy Spirit, and to manifestations of his gifts and power, individuals react in different ways. Some welcome what they see and hear immediately. When Jean was first taken to a charismatic service, she knew from the moment the worship band played the first chord that she had found what, like Maureen, she had been seeking all her life. Others need time to think and pray about it, perhaps just to wait and see, before committing themselves to what seems to be a dangerous novelty or perhaps a passing fad. Geoff and Jill were very suspicious when they first saw and heard manifestations of the Holy Spirit, but they were eventually touched by God's Spirit in life-changing ways. This process can take weeks, months or even years, and we should not give up on anyone.

Others, however, exhibit much more negative reactions to the manifest power of the Holy Spirit, ranging from abject fear to anger and rage. The reasons behind such negative reactions are many and complex, and in individual cases difficult or impossible to analyse. There is a simple fear of the supernatural, which is healthy in itself: 'The fear of the LORD is the beginning of wisdom' (Proverbs 9:10). For many people a demonstration of the gifts of the Holy Spirit may be the first time they have caught a glimpse of the reality of the power of God. A deeper understanding of the love of God is necessary to counteract this fear. People ought to be afraid of supernatural manifestations which do not come from God, more afraid than they often are. The power of Satan and his demons is real and terrible. Without the gift of discernment, however, people can easily shy away from everything supernatural. Assurance of the greater power of God and his constant goodness is necessary to allay people's justifiable fear of spooks.

There is also a common fear of emotion. When we are faced with extreme distress, especially when we are young, a common human reaction is to suppress the memory of the event and with it the unmanageable emotions. Not a few people are sitting on an emotional volcano within, or trying to keep the lid on a seething emotional cauldron. The Holy Spirit tends to cause these memories and emotions to come to the surface, because that is the way we find healing and wholeness. But that process can feel immensely threatening and some people run away from it rather than face the pain and humiliation involved in healing.

Fear often leads to anger, but anger arises from other sources too. People in a traditional church are there for different reasons. The best one is that through the worship and ministry of the church they have found God, and they value the forms through which they have found and continue to find him. Such people may be hurt and angry if the forms of worship and ministry to which they are accustomed are changed or taken away. This is the origin of the common resistance to guitars in church, and to the modern songs that go with them. The organ and the old hymns have been powerful means of mediating to people the presence of God and the truths of the Christian faith, and they do not want to lose them. The same is true of the formality and restraint of traditional liturgical worship. To those who are used to this type of service, the exuberance and freedom of so-called 'happy-clappy' worship is a threat to be resisted.

There are other people in church for less respectable reasons. The choir or the organist may be there for the love of church music rather than the love of God. The bell-ringers may be there for the love of bell-ringing. Others may be there for the love of the church's social life, the flower-arranging, the Mother's Union, the fundraising events, or simply for the idea of the village church; perhaps they have watched too many episodes of *The Vicar of Dibley*. These people react angrily if their church is suddenly hijacked by the Holy Spirit.

I have never heard of a traditional church, at least in the countryside, which has been renewed without a degree of conflict. In some cases, good management and the good hand of God upon that church may have successfully minimised the conflict. In other cases, bad management or implacable opposition have led to irrevocable splits and division. I have never heard of a renewal that was painless. If that is the case, then those setting out to lead a traditional church into renewal must first count the cost, and then decide on a strategy.

The cost is peace, in the church and in the parish. It is a high cost and a difficult one for the average Christian, especially the average Anglican, to accept. The prevailing ethos of the Church of England is that the chief function of bishops and clergy is to keep the peace. Confrontation is not encouraged. No one is right or wrong; everyone is entitled to their point of view, and the Church of England's job is to embrace them all. If only it were so! Jesus brought conflict – he would not have been popular in the Church of England. He sometimes went out of his way to be confrontational. No one who reads Matthew 23, with its curses of the scribes and Pharisees, can imagine that Jesus saw his function as keeping everybody happy. He said, 'Do not suppose that I have come to bring peace to the earth. I did not come to bring peace, but a sword' (Matthew 10:34). As the coming of Jesus in the flesh brought division, so today the coming of the Spirit of Jesus brings the same divisions, and that is the cost of renewal.

Those setting out on the road of congregational renewal must therefore do so, not in a spirit of timidity, but in the spirit of love, power and self-control (2 Timothy 1:7). It is not the role and calling of the church to please people, but to please God. If pleasing God means displeasing people, then we have to pluck up our courage and displease them. Just as no one can serve both God and Mammon, so no one can serve both God and popular opinion. So, with conflict over the renewal of the church in view, it is prudent to consider the options for dealing with it.

The first possibility is clearly to give up. Few would admit openly to such a defeatist attitude, but many end up there, either before or after fighting the battles. Many a vicar is simply waiting for the time to be right to introduce renewal; just at the moment, however, his people are not ready for it. The trouble is, they never will be. The softly, softly, slowly, slowly approach means that the progress of renewal is dictated by the opposition. With such an attitude renewal will never even start. Others, having adopted a bolder, more gung-ho approach, run into such heavy fire that they are beaten back and retire from the battlefield wounded or spiritually dead. Such men and women deserve sympathy. Like wounded soldiers they need to be healed, restored and encouraged to return to the fight, perhaps better prepared or better supported next time around. None of us can be sure we will not suffer the same fate. But God is merciful.

The second strategy for dealing with conflict over renewal is to take no prisoners and accept no surrender except an unconditional one. This means that in the end the only choice for members of the old church is to accept the renewal or leave. There is a hard logic about such a course, but it is unmerciful to human weakness, closes the door to the possibility of future change, and involves some uncharitable judgements about the reasons for people's opposition. We have looked at some of the many and varied reasons why there is opposition to renewal. While some of them can be ignored, others need to be handled with respect and compassion. Nonetheless, whatever intentions or strategies we start out with, we may find at the end of the day that we finish up in a position where people have either accepted the renewal or left.

The third strategy is compromise. It doesn't sound good in the context of the ministry of Jesus, but in the context of twenty-first-century Britain it sounds ideal. We take a bit of this and a bit of that – a bit of the old tradition, a bit of charismatic renewal, perhaps a bit of Taizé and a bit of Celtic spirituality, who knows, even a bit of Gregorian chant and the mysticism of the Desert Fathers, and behold, everyone is satisfied and happy. Usually the opposite is true. Those who have embraced renewal are still impatient with the constraints of traditionalism and further impatient with the diversions of spiritual dilettantism, while the traditionalists and the dilettanti continue to be irritated and threatened by the charismatics.

Perhaps the best strategy, the most peaceable and charitable one, the one that will cause the least conflict and aggravation, is separation – building a new (or renewed) church alongside the old (or traditional) one. Let the traditional services and life of the church go on without the threat of unwelcome change, while at another time and perhaps in another place there grows a new and renewed congregation with the freedom to be itself and to follow the vision God has given it. It will not be a perfect solution, nor will it prevent all conflict, but it may avoid the worst of it.

*   *   *

In our own two churches, St Nicholas's and St George's, I began by preaching Jesus and the baptism of the Holy Spirit. From the beginning I adopted the habit of calling people forward whenever I wanted them to respond in some definite way. Immediately, some Anglicans, used to being left alone with their own thoughts, began to feel uncomfortably challenged.

During my first Lent there, I taught more about the person and work of the Holy Spirit to those who wanted to hear, and we began to put into practice what we learned: the ministry of healing, the exercise of the gifts of the Spirit, including the gift of tongues. At first we explored the new ways of intimacy in worship and ministry in the power of the Holy Spirit at mid-week meetings. After a while, however, people who had been personally renewed in the Spirit and had experienced something more at Christian conferences outside the parish began to ask why we could not do more of 'that stuff' in the Sunday services. I was very happy to move in that direction. It was where I believed the church should go, and I now had a body of support for such changes.

Looking back through the retrospectoscope, I now wonder if that may have been a mistake. As our worship changed, step by step, we found ourselves faced with one disagreement after another. There was trouble about the guitars and the drums, about the new worship songs and the way we sang them, about dancing in church and about banners, about the public use of the gift of tongues, about words of knowledge, about the invocation of the Holy Spirit, about people laughing, crying and falling under the power of the Holy Spirit. We also stumbled over other issues which had been lying dormant in the church, including yoga, freemasonry and extramarital partnerships.

The trouble arose because not everyone in the church moved on spiritually at the same speed, or even moved on at all. We provided many opportunities for people to understand what we were doing and why we were doing it, but some always seemed to miss the teaching and the explanations, and some did not want to understand anyway.

We tried to regulate the pace of change so that we did not leave behind those who were willing but slow, while at the same time not allowing those who were hitting the brakes to stop the train altogether. Thus we lived for some seven years in a state of tension, a state which, I guess, is only too familiar to others in this situation. On the one hand there were the born-again, Spirit-filled charismatics crying, 'Faster, faster!' On the other hand there were the entrenched traditionalists saying, 'Stop, stop!' We made progress, because a majority in the congregations and the church councils were in favour of change. But we dragged with us, in both churches, a band of people who were constantly discontented with the way things were going. It was not, in the end, a comfortable time for anyone, and eventually the couplings snapped and the train came apart.

*   *   *

I think that, without clearly formulating the options, I had adopted the strategy of compromise. From the day we took the new things of the Spirit and tried to integrate them with the old things in the church services, we were always looking for ways of negotiating compromises between the charismatics and the traditionalists. Were I doing it all over again, I would try a different strategy from the beginning: separation. I would have encouraged the midweek meetings to grow into an alternative Sunday service, separate from the traditional services. I do not

believe that this would have saved us from all our troubles –
sooner or later there would have been jealousy and competition for prime time. But to anyone else embarking on this work
I would now say, build a new church alongside the old one.

3

Structural Renewal

In *Streams of Living Water* I wrote about a project to remove some of the pews and reorder St Nicholas's. I finished by saying:

> There were undoubtedly some who were living in hope that our new ways were just a passing fad. Rectors, with their idiosyncrasies, had come and gone, leaving the village church to go on much as before. This rector would go too, one day. But the removal of the pews was something different: a final good-bye. The pews were more than furniture; they were totems. Their removal would mean that there was no going back. A furniture-removal van at the church gate would be a prophetic sign that the Church was moving on.

In the event, the furniture removal van never arrived at the church gate, and that was a prophetic sign that the church was not moving on.

We had reached a point in the renewal of the village church where the congregation had risen to over a hundred, including a good number of children and young people. The medieval building itself and its Victorian furnishings were now a physical constraint on our activities and the development of our life and worship as a congregation. The nave and aisle of the church were filled with pews from wall to wall, fixed and

33

immovable. Eighteenth-century congregations were notoriously
inattentive to what the parson was saying, and sleeping was
one of the less distracting pastimes. Contemporary reports
speak of people whispering and giggling during the service as if
they were at the theatre. The Victorians, whether of an evangelical or Anglo-Catholic persuasion, took their religion much
more seriously than that, and pews were installed that made
people sit up straight and face the front. The Victorian clergy
were control freaks. Such were our pews at St Nicholas's!

The renewed congregation, however, did not always want to
sit up straight and face the front. Fellowship meals, whether as
part of the Alpha course or at the conclusion of a Sunday service, cannot be eaten in straight lines facing the front, with
everyone's plates on their knees. Children are notoriously
bored and restless in pews. If people wanted to stand and talk
to each other over a cup of coffee, they had to squeeze into the
aisles. Some people wanted, like King David, to express their
worship by dancing before the Lord. We often wanted to pray
for one another in little groups of three or four. All-age worship involved drama or some physical activity for the children
or young people. We needed to be able to move the furniture
and use the space that we had in the church in a variety of
more creative ways. Sitting up straight and facing the front is
fine for pupils being taught or lectured, but even schools had
long since moved away from such formal methods of learning,
and we had discovered that as a church we had many other
needs.

A scheme to remove some of the pews and open up the side
aisle was making steady progress through the various committees involved and had the overwhelming, if not unanimous,
support of the church council. If there was opposition to the
scheme in the council, it was as much because we were not
doing enough as because we were doing anything at all. We
were just about to publish the statutory public notices advertis-
ing the scheme, when without warning a letter was delivered to
every house in the village announcing a campaign to prevent it.

A recently retired resident of the parish had heard about our plans and was determined to oppose them by all means. He had with him a core of the worshippers who had for a long time been unhappy about the charismatic innovations and who had now found, in the pews, an issue over which they could finally make a stand. Moreover, there were many people out in the village who did not come to church from one year's end to another, but who were nevertheless scandalised at the thought that someone might be desecrating their church in such a way. They might not come to church often, but when they did they were sure they wanted to sit on a pew and not on a chair.

All of a sudden we were engulfed in a tidal wave of publicity and media interest. We might have been the first church in Britain to remove our pews, such was the commotion. National radio programmes, regional television, newspapers from the local to the national broadsheets, all ran features, many with photographs and background comment. Only slowly did I realise that we represented, in microcosm, movements which were affecting the wider church, and our situation enabled people to put a face to what were otherwise abstract ideas.

Eugene Ionescu wrote about the community of his childhood, 'Everyone and everything had a face. Religion had a face, the priest's face. Authority had a face, the mayor's or the local policeman's. Knowledge had a face, the schoolmaster's. Labour had a face, the blacksmith's. Everything was personalised, concrete.' Our village pews personalised and made concrete something that was happening throughout the church and throughout the country: a spiritual renewal which was affecting individuals, congregations and eventually the structures of the church.

In the glare of such publicity opinions polarised and attitudes became entrenched. At the end of six months it was clear that any change to the fabric and furnishings of St Nicholas's was going to involve a trial before a consistory court, with judges and barristers, and fees and expenses to match.

I thought and prayed much during this time, and tried to see through the smoke of gunfire to the real issues. This was not just about pews, obviously – it was about the whole movement of renewal, whether it could continue or whether it could be stopped. More than this, it was about power and authority – who in the church and the village ultimately called the shots? It was about the structures of the church in two senses of the word – the physical structures, the medieval stones and the Victorian woodwork, but also the institutional structures, how the church was governed and organised.

The full implications of the decisions we faced could not be foreseen, but I could foresee that going to court was unlikely to achieve anything. Win or lose, the costs would be enormous. I knew of PCCs which had been burdened for years with debts resulting from consistory courts. There were, moreover, many signs that we would actually lose such a case. Decisions in cases comparable to ours did not give me great cause for hope: most of the cards today are stacked in favour of conservation rather than change. If we were to lose the case in court, I was quite clear that it would not mean the end of the progress of renewal in the congregation. If the route of reordering the medieval church proved a dead end, we would simply have to go somewhere else. I was determined that, inside the parish church or outside it, we were going to find the freedom we needed to continue to change and grow. To move the people looked altogether easier than to move the pews.

So, one Sunday in June I announced from the pulpit that in six weeks' time I proposed to start a new service in the village community centre, half a mile down the road, for such as cared to attend. In the community centre there were no pews. Some years before, we had moved the Sunday morning services out of our neighbouring village church, St George's, while the heating system was being repaired. Now it was time to do the same thing for different reasons at St Nicholas's. The bishop agreed to the move, provided we retained a traditional Anglican service in the parish church, something which neither I nor my colleagues had any objection to doing. Thus, in July 1996, the train was uncoupled: the renewed part of the congregation, about 90 people, went on by itself to worship in the community centre, while the more traditional part, perhaps 40 to 50 people, stayed on in the parish church.

This was by no means a painless solution to the problem. For some of those who left the parish church, the parting broke ties which went back a very long way. This was a village church in which some of the congregation had been baptised and married, where they had worshipped all their lives, and their fathers before them. In many cases their ancestors were buried in the churchyard. This place *was* church for them. It says a lot for the strength of their new-found relationship with God that they were prepared to make the break at all. Many, like David and his men, left Jerusalem and went up the Mount of Olives into exile weeping (2 Samuel 15:30). Some people found themselves uncertain which way to go and it took months, and in some cases years, for people finally to sort themselves out. Some couples were divided, one partner going one way, one partner the other.

No one who made the break looked back, however. Some wondered initially whether God could be found anywhere except in the medieval parish church, but discovered the truth that wherever two or three are gathered in his name, Jesus is there in the midst of them. We had all solemnly declared for years that of course the church was people and not buildings; now we were putting our theology to the test and finding to our delight that it was true. Immediately we found a new freedom in worship, in prayer, in fellowship together. There was a new joy and sense of expectation about our services and meetings. New people, who had been part of neither parish church, began to join us, some from our own villages, some from outside them, some Anglicans, some Baptists, some Pentecostals, some from no church background whatsoever.

While some of those who stayed behind were glad to see the charismatics go, others were genuinely sad and grieved, as we all did, over the separation. This was a sort of divorce. Coming as it did at the end of a difficult relationship, it was in many ways a relief, but there was pain on both sides.

For some months I held out the hope that the situation might yet be resolved and there might be reconciliation, but that was not to be. There followed three years of uneasy separation. I remained the rector of the two parish churches, now with an additional responsibility for a third, separate congregation. This congregation eventually named itself the Fountain of Life.

The status of the Fountain of Life in law was unclear. Technically it remained subordinate to the church council of St Nicholas's and we arranged an informal system of shared representation on this council. The diocesan authorities were not particularly happy at this turn of affairs (who was?), but they worked with us to try to find a solution to the legal and technical problems. Here was a Church of England congregation under a Church of England priest, but it was clearly not a parish church. How could that be? The structure of the Church of England is strictly geographical and parochial. There might be ancient anomalies such as royal peculiars and proprietary chapels, but no one was eager to multiply these. In time we discovered that the Fountain of Life was not unique in the contemporary Church of England; there were a few similar nonparochial congregations in other parts of the country, some of which had originated as more deliberate church plants, while others had arisen out of situations similar to ours. Some of them were exploring the concept of an extraparochial place.

Three years after our first separation, the tenuous links still holding the three churches together finally broke apart. My colleagues and I had been happy to continue to minister to all three congregations in the ways that were acceptable to them. I still enjoyed the quietness and stillness of an early morning Communion service out of the Book of Common Prayer. I still appreciated the strength and depth of many of the old hymns. But increasingly the two traditional congregations felt that my heart lay with the Fountain of Life and not with them, and I guess they were right. I had to admit that, if I were forced to choose, I would choose the renewed charismatic church rather than the traditional ones. In July 1999 I was forced to choose.

The two traditional church councils met then and asked me to resign. They had no power to fire me, but ministry is a two-way process: it has to be both given and received. If these churches were no longer willing to receive my ministry, it was time for me to go. So, on the 31st December 1999, I went. I ceased to be the rector of the two parish churches, and steps were taken to appoint a successor. I was relicensed some months later by the bishop, as a curate with special responsibility for the Fountain of Life. My wife and I moved out of the old rectory and the diocesan authorities purchased a new house for us on the outskirts of the village.

Meanwhile, the Fountain of Life had been discovering not just the advantages of being free from the old building, but also the disadvantages of having no building at all. The community centre in which we met on Sundays admirably fulfilled our requirements, but anyone who has planted a church in secular premises knows the cost in terms of time and energy involved in setting up and taking everything down every Sunday. Teams of people began to arrive an hour and a half before the service was due to begin, to set up a sound system, to carry chairs and tables, to plug in and tune up, to fill urns, to set out children's materials and a crèche corner. Box after box of equipment was heaved in, and afterwards everything was heaved out again. For those most heavily involved, a morning service occupied over four hours' work.

The community centres in both our villages are, of course, in almost continuous use at other times of the week for other community activities – Women's Institute, Brownies, youth club, senior citizens' activities, badminton, bridge, line-dancing, kick-boxing and much more. So we were continually looking for venues for midweek activities, including prayer meetings, Alpha courses, band practice, day conferences, mothers and toddlers groups, and youth activities. Every new initiative meant a new search for a suitable room or hall.

From the early days some people had said, 'What we need is a purpose-built worship centre.' I had taken a good deal of convincing. Having just escaped from the problems of one building, I was not easily persuaded that we wanted to saddle ourselves with the problems of another. Over a period of time, however, the sheer practicalities, and what I took to be clear signs from God, persuaded me that we did need to look for a facility of our own. Buildings are indeed facilities: they facilitate the mission of the church. If they cease to facilitate that mission and begin to hinder it, as the old church had done, then it is time to walk away from them. We had done that, but the need for facilities still remained.

We began the search for a possible building, or a site on which to build one. A member of the Fountain of Life who was also a farmer in the parish offered us land on which to build, but after a long-drawn-out process, our planning application was refused. Suitable sites or suitable buildings for such a use in a rural area are few and far between. Again the cards are stacked in favour of conservation rather than development. Eventually we were offered the opportunity to buy the local garage for conversion to a worship centre. This time the planning application was granted without objection, and no one quarrelled with us about the site. A church gift day raised the astonishing sum of £292,000, which, although not sufficient in itself to complete the project, gave us more than enough confidence to believe that God was in it, and to set off down the road of purchase and conversion with an assurance that the remainder of the necessary money would also be forthcoming. So there we were, doing what I had never imagined I would be doing so literally – building a new church alongside an old one.

*   *   *

When I first led the renewed congregation out of the parish church, I had some inkling that what we were doing was seismic. And so it was, in terms of the structures of the Church of England. It has made us ask questions about aspects of the church that seemed previously and still seem to many to be unquestionable – our attitude to our heritage of ancient buildings, the relationship of the church to the community, the parish system itself, the constitution of the Church of England, and its future. The remainder of this book outlines the exploration of these questions which our situation has forced us to undertake. The Fountain of Life is either a rogue mutation which, like all such mutations, will quickly become extinct, or it is the future of the Church of England. Only time will tell which it is.

PART TWO

Mission and Maintenance

Mission and Maintenance

4

Mission

> [Jesus] said to them, 'Go into all the world and preach the good news to all creation. Whoever believes and is baptised will be saved, but whoever does not believe will be condemned . . .' Then the disciples went out and preached everywhere, and the Lord worked with them and confirmed his word by the signs that accompanied it. (Mark 16:15–16, 20)

That is the church in mission mode. As the Father sent Jesus into one small corner of the world, so Jesus sent his disciples out into all the world, to make known the good news. The fundamental understanding energising this mission is that there is a salvation to be found through faith in the name of Jesus which cannot be found in any other name. This is confirmed by the words of Jesus, 'No-one comes to the Father except through me' (John 14:6), and by the words of the apostle Peter, 'Salvation is found in no-one else, for there is no other name under heaven given to men by which we must be saved' (Acts 4:12). If it were possible to come into a right relationship with God in any other way, then the sufferings of Jesus were superfluous, the cross was in vain.

In the earliest years, the church's mission was wonderfully directed by the Holy Spirit. Jesus indicated what the course of the mission would be when he said, 'You will be my witnesses in Jerusalem, and in all Judea and Samaria, and to the ends of the earth' (Acts 1:8). The book of Acts is the story of how that commission was fulfilled, and it is clear that it was not fulfilled according to the careful planning or foresight of the apostles. The apostles remained in Jerusalem not only before the Day of Pentecost but also after it, faithfully labouring in preaching, teaching and building up the church in the city. It was the persecution that arose after the stoning of Stephen that drove the believers out of Jerusalem into Judea and Samaria (Acts 8:1) – and because they preached the word wherever they went (8:4), the mission of the church progressed into those regions, as Jesus had foretold.

The first breakthrough into the Gentile world was no less a sovereign work of God. The supernatural revelations that God gave to a Roman centurion, Cornelius, and to the apostle Peter were the keys that opened the door to the Gentiles (Acts 10). The waves of believers rolling out from Jerusalem after the death of Stephen also reached Antioch, where the gospel was preached to Greeks as well as Jews, a move for which God had prepared the church through Peter's experience in Caesarea (Acts 11). It was from this same city of Syrian Antioch that Paul and Barnabas were sent out, again in response to the prophetic guidance of the Holy Spirit, to spread abroad the good news of what God had done in Palestine for the salvation of the world.

If we may suppose that Paul's hope of visiting Spain was fulfilled (Romans 15:24) between the end of the story in the book of Acts and his traditional martyrdom in Rome, then before the generation of the first apostles had passed away the gospel had already been preached (in modern terms) in the Middle East, Turkey, Greece, Yugoslavia, Italy, France, Spain, North Africa and possibly even India and the Far East. Not bad for one generation! That was the church in missionary mode.

The momentum hardly faltered after the death of the apostles. The gospel continued to spread throughout the Roman Empire and beyond. The infant churches planted by the apostles grew as the believers multiplied, and these churches in turn planted new ones in every place. Even by the time of the Emperor Nero and the great fire of Rome in AD 64, the Christians were a significant minority worth persecuting. By AD 112 the younger Pliny was asking for guidance from the Emperor Trajan because Christianity was spreading from the towns to the countryside, and the pagan temples were becoming deserted. Persecution was at first sporadic, rather than systematic, but where it occurred it only seemed to reinforce the power of the believers' testimony. 'The blood of the martyrs is the seed of the Church,' wrote Tertullian in AD 200.

More serious persecution was to follow in the reigns of later emperors, Decius (AD 250), Valerian (AD 258) and Diocletian (AD 305), but by this time the Christians were simply too numerous and the church too strong to be wiped out. Even in AD 200 Tertullian had been able to boast to the Romans, 'We Christians arose but yesterday, and yet we fill everything you have – cities, tenements, forts, towns, exchanges, yes! and camps, tribes, palaces, senate, forum.'

None of this was accomplished by great campaigns or special efforts. Michael Green, writing about evangelism in the early church, says,

> Evangelism today is often associated with the great public meeting. It is a remarkable fact that the early Church seems to have made very little use of this method of commending the gospel . . . The emphasis lay on home and personal evangelism . . . House meetings of various sorts and personal conversations between individuals played a very prominent part in the progress of the gospel in ancient times. The hospitality and even the decoration of their homes, their chance conversations indoors or in the open air, visiting, open-air preaching, addresses in church and synagogue, arguments in the market place and the philosophical school, personal testimony, letter writing and the explanation of Scripture were all used to further the supreme aim which these early Christians cherished, of making Christ known to others.[1]

1 Michael Green, *Evangelism in the Early Church* (Hodder & Stoughton, 1970), pp. 278–9.

That was the church in missionary mode.

The effectiveness of such witness is demonstrated in the simple historical fact that less than 300 years after the death of Jesus the mighty Roman emperor himself bowed before the power of the cross: in AD 312 Constantine decided that if the Empire could not beat the Christians, he had better join them. The conversion of Constantine is a momentous event in the history of the church. To Christians who so recently had suffered such savage persecution, Constantine's Edict of Milan, proclaiming not just toleration but favour towards the church, must have seemed the answer to their prayers. How could they foresee that the patronage of the state was going to be a very mixed blessing?

All of a sudden Christians were free from the fear of imprisonment and death, and found themselves living under the special favour and protection of the state. But that brought other temptations and dangers, which the church was ill-prepared to resist. Large numbers of nominal Christians joined the church because of the social and legal privileges that believers, especially the clergy, now enjoyed. Pagan customs were assimilated into Christian festivals: Saturnalia became Christmas without ever losing its character of a boozy midwinter binge. The church became caught up in a new worldliness of silver and gold, sumptuous vestments and ornate basilicas. Soon the emperor, who still managed to combine the worship of the sun with the worship of the Son of God (after all, both were worshipped on Sunday), was insisting that he himself should be involved in determining matters of church discipline and doctrine. With hindsight we can see that the conversion of Constantine meant that the state, having failed to prevent the growth of the church, then took the church over. It was not necessary to evangelise the citizens of Rome any more; the pressures of social conformity and worldly advantage were sufficient to bring them in.

In many ways this is the beginning of a new phase in the church's existence: Christendom, of which I shall have more to say later. Just as the missionary endeavour of the church within the Roman Empire seemed to have been triumphantly successful, so God provided new challenges for the church's mission. Just as the Roman Empire, the old enemy of the church, seemed to have become a friend, the Lord raised up new foes, to be both resisted and evangelised. In AD 248 the Roman Empire had suffered the first serious invasion of a barbarian tribe from Central Europe, the Goths. Over the next few centuries these mysterious and violent waves of ethnic migration became more and more frequent and devastating. Under these incessant attacks the Empire began to crumble; Rome itself was sacked in 410, and Western Europe was progressively overrun by hordes that were neither Christian nor civilised.

If the Roman Empire crumbled, however, the church did not. Somehow, over the next 500 years, the so-called Dark Ages, the church managed not only to survive, but also to evangelise these barbarian tribes. Largely through the monasteries, the church transmitted to them the rudiments of Christianity and the rudiments of civilisation and learning. A conversion as momentous for the history of Europe as the conversion of Constantine was that of Clovis, king of the Franks, in AD 496.

One by one these new people groups were brought into contact with the Christian message. Often, once more, it was the blood of the martyrs that was the seed of the church. Often the heathen kings were converted first – like Ethelbert, the Anglo-Saxon king of Kent in AD 597. Mass conversions, obviously of a superficial nature, would then follow among their people. The missionaries were now operating in a very different culture and society from those who first took the gospel to the pluralistic and sophisticated world of ancient Rome.

Mass conversions were not necessarily forced conversions, however. Bede records that, on the arrival of Augustine and the missionaries from Rome, Ethelbert received them hospitably and gave them permission to preach in his kingdom 'and win any people you can to your religion'. Bede goes on:

At length the king himself, among others, edified by the pure lives of these holy men and their gladdening promises, the truth of which they confirmed by many miracles, believed and was baptised. Thenceforward great numbers gathered each day to hear the word of God, forsaking their heathen rites and entering the unity of Christ's holy Church as believers. While the king was pleased at their faith and conversion, it is said that he would not compel anyone to accept Christianity; for he had learned from his instructors and guides to salvation that the service of Christ must be accepted freely and not under compulsion.[2]

Nevertheless, the example of the king or chieftain was often sufficient to persuade large numbers of their subjects to accept baptism and at least a nominal adherence to the new faith. This was a form of society in which the notions of individual rights and individual choice featured much less than notions of communal or tribal solidarity. The missionaries themselves were not unaware of the shallowness of such mass conversions and the best of them, like Cuthbert, laboured diligently in preaching and teaching among these rude converts.

Cuthbert used mainly to visit and preach in the villages that lay far distant among high and inaccessible mountains, which others feared to visit and whose barbarity and squalor daunted other teachers. Cuthbert, however, gladly undertook this pious task, and taught with such patience and skill that when he left the monastery it would sometimes be a week, sometimes two or three, and occasionally an entire month, before he returned home, after staying in the mountains to guide the peasants heavenward by his teaching and virtuous example.[3]

Nor should we suppose that such endeavours were fruitless. A historian of Anglo-Saxon England, Hunter Blair, has given this as his considered opinion: 'There are signs that attitudes

---

2 Bede, *A History of the English Church and People I 26* (Penguin, 1955), p. 71.
3 Ibid, *IV 27*, p. 260.

towards earthly kingship were markedly affected by Christian teaching during the eighth century.'[4]

It was from the British Isles themselves that some of the greatest missionaries set out again to evangelise the rest of Europe. When Patrick set sail for Ireland he began a train of events which profoundly influenced the whole of Europe. In the fifth and sixth centuries Irish monks like Columbanus travelled far and wide, through France, Switzerland and Italy. From Ireland also came Columba, from whose monastery on Iona missionaries evangelised both Scotland and northern England. In the seventh and eighth centuries it was Anglo-Saxon missionaries like Willibrord and Boniface who brought the gospel to Holland and Germany.

*   *   *

Thus we may say that for roughly a thousand years the church remained in what we have called 'missionary mode': outward looking, fired by zeal for the salvation of souls, conscious of the surrounding darkness, and motivated by the Great Commission of Jesus Christ. As the first millennium drew to a close, however, there came again a sense that the job had been done. Pagan Europe seemed to have been won a second time for Christ; heathendom had finally become Christendom. Somewhere around AD 1000 the church changed out of missionary mode and into maintenance mode. The church in the second millennium, the church as most of us have experienced it in the West, has been just that: the church functioning in Christendom or maintenance mode.

---

4 P. Hunter Blair, *Northumbria in the Days of Bede* (Book Club Associates, London, 1976), p. 58.

5

Maintenance

Christendom was a geographical area, a state of mind, a theory and a polity. It was that area of the world which, in the Middle Ages, was identified as Christian, by comparison with the world beyond. This area consisted more or less of what we now call Western Europe. As far as anyone knew, everywhere to the south was Muslim, from Spain, across North Africa and through the Middle East as far as Turkey. To the east of Europe were the barbarian hordes which had overthrown the Roman Empire and which constantly threatened new eruptions of peril. To the north dwelled the Vikings, who ruled and rode the seas and raided Christian countries with equally unpredictable brutality. To the west there was only the great, wide sea, and the edge of the world.

Within this pale lived together those tribes and peoples who had settled down in the West during the Dark Ages and had been, at least superficially, Christianised by the heroic and tireless labours of missionaries and monks. Still looking to Rome as the fountainhead of civilisation and of authority in the church, these peoples were heirs to a culture and a religion which united them across the boundaries of tribe, language and embryonic nationhood. For nearly a thousand years their rulers relied on the monasteries to provide them with men of letters and learning for the administration of the state as well as the church – clergymen and clerks were one and the same thing. The only civilisation that medieval Europe knew was one which had been mediated to it by the Christian church. Throughout the Middle Ages Latin was the common language, not only of worship and the business of the church, but also of education, the law, commerce and diplomacy. People travelled freely across Europe in a way that is only now once again becoming possible and commonplace with the development of the European Union; they were the subjects not so much of particular nations, but of Christendom.

Throughout the Middle Ages, Christendom felt itself to be under siege. This is how the twelfth-century chronicler William of Malmesbury described the situation as he perceived it:

> The world is not evenly divided. Of its three parts, our enemies hold Asia as their hereditary home. Yet here formerly our Faith put out its branches; here all the Apostles save two met their deaths. But now the Christians of those parts, if there are any left, squeeze a bare subsistence from the soil and pay tribute to their enemies, looking to us with silent longing for the liberty they have lost. Africa too, the second part of the world, has been held by our enemies by force of arms for two hundred years and more, a danger to Christendom all the greater because it formerly sustained the brightest spirits. Thirdly, there is Europe, the remaining region of the world. Of this region we Christians inhabit only a part, for who will give the name of Christians to those barbarians who live in the remote islands and seek their living on the icy ocean as if they were whales? This little portion of the world which is ours is pressed upon by warlike Turks and Saracens: for three hundred years they have held Spain and they live in hope of devouring the rest.[1]

For the first 300 years of its history, the church had relied on the strength and protection of God alone. It was often threat-

---

1 Quoted by R. W. Southern, *The Making of the Middle Ages* (Arrow, 1959), p. 74

ened and persecuted, but it grew. Ever since the conversion of Constantine, however, the church had come to rely on worldly armies and princes for its protection, a protection without which the church no longer believed that it could survive.

Relying now on worldly rulers and the power of the sword, the church – in the form of the pope and his bishops – was inexorably drawn into the power struggles and power politics of medieval Europe. The corruption of the church which this entailed was shameful; the Spirit of the gospel was sacrificed to a spirit of holy war on the church's enemies, with catastrophic results; the priorities and focus of the church's life were diverted into enterprises which ended up disgracing the name of Jesus. The Crusades epitomise this new spirit: the aim of the church was no longer to convert the infidels but to vanquish them in battle. The Christians had cast away the weapons of righteousness with which they had previously demolished the strongholds of pride and pretension, and had taken up the weapons of the world (2 Corinthians 10:3–5).

As in all such societies under siege, there was also the fear of the enemy within. Jews were the subject of sporadic but vicious pogroms and persecution. As the frontiers of Christian Spain were enlarged, so both Muslims and Jews were forcibly baptised. There was going to be no room for dissent, nor for plurality of beliefs or opinions, inside medieval Europe. Those who departed from the orthodox faith, like the Albigensians, were not just persuaded to renounce their errors by the Inquisition, but were put to death if they refused to do so. Medieval Christendom was not an open society, but a closed and totalitarian one.[2]

This mentality was not significantly altered by the Reformation. Those states which embraced one form of Protestantism or another were no more liberal than those which remained Catholic: only one form of religion could be

---

2 Karl Popper, *The Open Society and its Enemies* (Routledge, 1966).

tolerated in any one place. In Spain everyone must be a Catholic; in Geneva everyone must be a Calvinist; in England everyone must be an Anglican; in Europe everyone must still be a Christian, even though Christendom was now shattered into many different pieces. A geographical fact became a state of mind for all the peoples of Europe, of all ranks and classes, from the Pope to the peasant, from the king to the carver: one was a Christian not by personal choice but by one's birth in the lands of Christendom. We were Christians because we were not Turks or Jews or heathens, living out there on the dim perimeter of the known world. Christian simply meant 'us' as opposed to 'them'.

Under this regime every citizen of Europe was formally obliged to be a member of the church. Everyone was baptised at birth; everyone was supposed to be in church on Sundays for worship; every bridegroom was supposed to bring his bride to the church for the solemnisation of their marriage; and everyone, except the suicides and the excommunicated, was buried in the churchyard with Christian funeral rites. The church provided everyone with the necessary mechanisms for attaining salvation and for avoiding the terrifying pains of hell. With the Reformation and the passage of time, the understanding of the mechanisms changed. For Catholics, receiving the correct sacraments was the mechanism; for Protestants, believing the correct doctrines was the mechanism; for ordinary Englishmen, living the correct sort of life became the mechanism. But the mentality of Christendom lived on in them all: we might be good Christians or bad Christians, but we were all Christians.

Very early on, indeed as early as the conversion of Constantine, a false and fatal identification was made between the Christian nations of Europe and the Old Testament nation of Israel. The kings and emperors of Europe were identified as the successors of David and Solomon, the anointed heads of God's chosen people. From the coronation of Charlemagne on Christmas Day AD 800 to the coronation of Queen Elizabeth in London in 1953, the Christian rulers of Europe have been anointed with oil and consecrated in the name of Christ, not only to do justice and love mercy, but to extirpate heresy and defend the faith. An anonymous writer of the eleventh century expressed the theory of kingship common to Christendom: 'Kings and priests have a common unction of holy oil, a common spirit of sanctification, a common quality of benediction, the name and power of God and Christ in common.' Not for nothing is the anthem sung at coronations in Westminster Abbey: 'Zadok the priest and Nathan the prophet anointed Solomon king.'

In Christendom, church and state are the same body of people, their souls ruled over by the church, their bodies by the state. Although popes and rulers contended for centuries for supremacy over one another, all agreed that they were but the two arms of the body politic, the temporal arm and the spiritual arm. According to this understanding, the church prescribed what the laws should be, at least the laws governing religion, and the princes enforced them. Princes, of course, had their own fish to fry, but looked to the church for justification and for God's blessing on all their enterprises. This was the theory and the nature of a political collusion which seemed to serve the interests of both church and state for a large part of the medieval and modern eras in Europe. The church acquired earthly power and protection in a hostile world; rulers acquired legitimation and the blessing of God, even on their mutual hostilities.

As we have seen already, it was not the Reformation that changed this understanding of church and society, although it introduced an element of plurality into Christendom which had not been there before. Even within the Church of England, that most comprehensive and mild of the churches of the Reformation, Richard Hooker could still write at the end of the sixteenth century:

We hold, that seeing there is not any man of the Church of England but the same man is also a member of the commonwealth; nor any man a member of the commonwealth, which is not also of the Church of England . . . no person appertaining to the one can be denied to be also of the other.[3]

It was not until the eighteenth century that theories of the 'rights of man' began to challenge this understanding of the unity of church and state. It can be argued, as Larry Siedentop has recently done,[4] that the idea of the rights of the individual over against society has Christian roots; that it has arisen and could only have arisen in a Christian culture; and that, in fact, it will not survive outside a Christian culture. But such ideas arose, in both Europe and America, as a reaction to the religious wars of the seventeenth century and the savage persecutions which state churches of every kind inflicted on their dissidents. John Adams, one of the founding fathers of the United States of America, made it clear that the cause of freedom meant freedom from the tyrannies of both church and state.

Under the execrable race of the Stuarts [kings of seventeenth-century England], the struggle between the people and the confederacy of temporal and spiritual tyranny became formidable, violent and bloody. It was this great struggle that peopled America. It was not religion alone, as was commonly supposed, but it was a love of universal liberty, and a hatred, a dread, a horror of the internal confederacy of ecclesiastical, hierarchical, and despotic rulers that projected, conducted and accomplished the settlement of America.[5]

This is an assertion of human individuality over against the absolute claims of both church and state. It was the beginning

---

3 Richard Hooker, *Of the Laws of Ecclesiastical Polity*, Book VIII (Oxford, 1863), p. 330.

4 Larry Siedentop, *Democracy in Europe* (Allen Lane, 2000).

5 John Adams, *Dissertation on the Canon and Feudal Law*, 1765. Quoted by Paul Johnson, *A History of Christianity* (Weidenfeld and Nicholson, 1976), p. 425.

of the ideas of religious toleration in the state, and of the church as a voluntary association, of the untangling of the medieval synthesis which had dominated the lives and minds of Europeans for nearly a thousand years.

In England and France, thinkers like Locke and Voltaire had begun the process of thinking the unthinkable and saying the unsayable in their writings. But it was in the colonies of the New World that the new principles of religious pluralism and individual freedom of conscience were first comprehensively put into practice. After the American War of Independence, the First Amendment in the Bill of Rights 1791 enshrined for the first time the principle of freedom of religion. In one way and another, the constitutions of all the European states which once formed Christendom were modified in a similar sense during the eighteenth and nineteenth centuries – in France violently as a result of the French Revolution, in England more gradually by the Acts of Parliament emancipating Catholics and dissenters from their civil disabilities.

Today freedom of religion, involving an individual's right to believe and practise any religion or none, is guaranteed by law in every part of ancient Christendom. There are, however, still many relics of the old regime, not just in the constitutions of European states and churches, but also in the minds of many Western Christians. In England, as in the countries of Scandinavia, one church still enjoys a privileged position in relation to the state. The one person in England who is not free to choose his or her own religious faith is the sovereign, who must still by law be a member of the Church of England. Likewise, the constitution of the church still reflects many of the presuppositions of Christendom. Anyone resident in the parish still has the right to be married in the parish church, to have their infants baptised there, and to be buried in the churchyard, regardless of their actual beliefs and practices. Even in the USA, what is an atheistic American to make of his money, which still declares 'In God we trust'?

* * *

Such constitutional relics may seem insignificant enough, but they are tied to a persistent pattern of thinking which also derives from Christendom, and which, in the modern world, leads to a sort of Christian schizophrenia. With one half of our minds we recognise the rights of individuals to freedom of religious belief and association; with the other half we hang on to the fond notion that everyone in the country is really a Christian, a backslidden or deviant Christian perhaps, but nevertheless someone who should continue to enjoy many of the rights and privileges of church membership. With one half of our minds we recognise that the proportion of people who actively practise the Christian faith in most European countries is below 10 per cent and declining all the time; with the other half we hanker after the old idea that our countries are still Christian countries and our continent the Christian continent. We are thus prevented from realising that, in what used to be Christendom, we now once again face not a maintenance but a missionary situation.

The revival of a missionary perspective and of missionary fervour in the eighteenth and nineteenth centuries is itself instructive in this regard. What stimulated the new missionary endeavours was the opening up through exploration and trade of those lands beyond the frontiers of Christendom which had always been recognised as heathen: India and Africa, the Orient and the South Seas. In spite of, or perhaps because of, the evangelical revivals of the eighteenth and nineteenth centuries in Europe and America, there was no comparable reawakening of the churches to the need for missionary work at home. So today, despite the indisputable evidence of long-term statistical decline, despite the Christian churches' manifest loss of influence in society, despite the almost complete secularisation of European culture, despite widespread ignorance of even the most basic facts about Christianity, despite the almost universal acceptance of moral relativism, churches and people remain blind to the fact that twenty-first-century Europe is probably now the most unevangelised continent on earth. We still think in our collective memory that we are all Christians, and that mission must mean 'them out there'. Whatever our conscious minds tell us about the present situation, the church in the West is still locked into maintenance mode. We desperately need a paradigm shift in our thinking, and corresponding changes in the structures of the church – changes which are more far-reaching than we think.

6

From Maintenance to Mission

In 1975 the Church of England Bishop of Lincoln called on his diocese to 'move from maintenance to mission at every level of diocesan life'. A report was presented to the diocesan synod which outlined the challenges facing the church in the last quarter of the twentieth century and reminded the church that in every age it was called to mission. Parishes and deaneries were urged to transfer their efforts away from maintenance and renew their focus on mission. The synod was pleased to receive the report, but the substantive motions that it passed in response betrayed the real preoccupations of the church at that time.

The first motion resolved to reduce the establishment of stipendiary ministers in the diocese and to make arrangements for the redeployment of those who remained. This was not the first nor the last reduction and redeployment of this sort. As a result of both decreasing numbers of ministers and decreasing financial resources to pay them, pastoral reorganisation has become a regular feature of life in both the urban and the rural church. The second motion urged parishes to pay the working expenses of their ministers. The third motion initiated a scheme to train and authorise a variety of lay ministers. In the event, this last became a scheme to ordain ministers put forward by and trained in the local churches: 'ordained local ministry'.

Even at that stage it should have been plain that these resolutions had very little to do with mission, and everything to do with a galloping failure even to maintain the status quo. The end result, in spite of the brave words and the synod's initiatives, was that the decline of the church in the diocese, and its failure in the field of maintenance, let alone in the field of mission, continued unabated. The move from maintenance to mission simply did not happen.

In 1989 the Church of England Bishop of Norwich called on his church to 'move forward'. There were three areas in which he perceived the need for change: 'change from maintenance to mission; change from dependence on the clergy to reliance on the laity; change from centralisation to a focus on what is local'. Expanding on the move from maintenance to mission, the bishop continued:

> I see lay people faithful in their worship, though in tiny congregations. I see clergy faithfully ministering to large numbers of people and large geographical areas. I see clergy and laity together faithful in their responsibilities, maintaining the life of the Church and shouldering huge burdens in the upkeep of church buildings.

Then he warned:

> We have been dominated for a long time by a kind of defensive mentality, by the need to maintain the Church, to keep numbers going in congregations, to keep our buildings in good repair, to maintain the strength of the parochial ministry. We have worked harder and harder, not to grow, but to prevent the Church from losing too much ground.

He concluded, 'The overwhelming priority for us, must be Mission. We have been faithful in maintenance, in holding the line. The time, I believe, is right for change, for a shift to mission controlling our affairs rather than maintenance.'[1]

For someone who had lived through the previous exercise in

---

1 Peter Nott, *Moving Forward* (Diocese of Norwich, 1989).

the diocese of Lincoln in 1975, to come in at the beginning of this one in the diocese of Norwich in 1989 was like the experience that used to befall cinema-goers in the days before separate performances. In those days it was quite common to come into the cinema about halfway through the B feature, to see the main film and then to stay on while the B feature came round again. Halfway through, the pictures began to seem surprisingly familiar, and one would get up and slide out: one already knew the rest of the story. So it was for me, when I arrived in the diocese of Norwich at this point. I knew the story and, unhappily, I knew the ending of this particular saga. I was not mistaken.

When the time came for the bishop to retire, he wrote a sort of end-of-term report on his episcopate and reviewed the achievements of the eight years since his initial document about 'moving forward'. Reviewing the progress made in changing from maintenance to mission, his first observations were about the state of the medieval buildings:

> We have travelled a long way on the journey of church restoration . . . Not only are our churches in a better state of repair than they have been since the middle ages, but we are 70% along the way to complete restoration. I believe, as I have often said, that our generation in this diocese is called by God to give ourselves to this work of restoration.[2]

He did go on, 'Dedication to the church building is not incompatible with evangelism. It is not a matter of mere maintenance.' But it is a sad reflection on the outcome of the bishop's strategic call for a move from maintenance to mission eight years previously, that the most tangible evidence he could produce for the success of that call was that the old buildings were better maintained than ever before. Meanwhile, the numbers of people attending these ancient churches had continued to fall inexorably.

---

2 Peter Nott, *Moving Forward III* (Diocese of Norwich, 1996), p. 12.

I have not told the story of my experience in these two dioceses in order to pour scorn on the two bishops. Far from it. I have no doubt at all that both of them had a very realistic perception of the problems facing the church at the end of the twentieth century, and also that both of them put their finger on the only solution, to move from maintenance to mission. The fact that both failed to move their clergy and people in the desired direction says to me, not that they were mistaken in the attempt, nor that they were anything other than sincere and wholehearted in their aim, but that there were, and are, obstacles in the way of such a move much greater than appeared at first sight. There is a spiritual obstacle to be addressed, and then there are structural obstacles, which can be even more obstinate.

In 1995 Robert Warren, the Church of England's National Officer for Evangelism, wrote a very perceptive booklet entitled *Building Missionary Congregations*. In it he identified the congregation as the primary agent of mission. He suggested that the single most important factor in evangelism was a local church demonstrating the gospel. Indeed, Robert Warren would summarise the gospel for the twenty-first century in three sentences: 'God's way of being human has been revealed in Jesus. It is available to all, through the Holy Spirit. It is now being demonstrated in a church near you.'[3]

If that last sentence were always true, it would be good news indeed. But that is the first problem. Spiritually speaking, the church in inherited, Christendom, maintenance mode is a long way from the church as it needs to be if it is to function in mission mode. This is the first – unperceived – obstacle to the church making the transition from one mode to the other. The Bishop of Norwich commented in 1997, 'There is widespread concern for evangelism. Parishioners do not always use that language, but the concern is there. "We must find ways to bring more people into church" is a common sentiment.' It is indeed,

---

3 Robert Warren, *Building Missionary Congregations* (Church House, 1995), p. 22.

but it is the church still functioning spiritually in maintenance mode, not in mission mode.

Once again, just as the actual resolutions of the Lincoln diocesan synod in 1975 did not really address the substance of the debate, but were more indicative of where the church's priorities really lay, so a true idea of where the priorities of the church in Norfolk actually lie can be deduced from an issue of the diocesan newsletter. There is indeed a desire to bring more people into church, but the preferred ways of doing so are clearly flower festivals and concerts. Three pages of a typical summer edition are dedicated to small advertisements from the parishes, which include 17 flower festivals, 13 concerts, and a variety of other fundraising activities, down to a teddy bear parachute jump! The proverbial Martian landing in Norfolk could be forgiven for thinking that Jesus had said, 'Go into all the world and organise flower festivals.' Robin Greenwood is justified in saying, 'For the majority of people in this country our churches are irrelevant, peripheral and seemingly only concerned with their own trivial pursuits.'[4] The first change that has to be made in moving the church from maintenance to mission is a spiritual one.

The following table illustrates the difference, spiritually, between the church in these two modes today. The two columns indicate the values of the different modes of church life, and the different emphases which the church will place on various aspects of its activities. It may well be that the values and emphases are not always mutually exclusive – indeed, there may be strong connections between each pair of values. Nevertheless, there are radical differences in these values and emphases; they are not simply saying the same things in different language.

---

4 Robin Greenwood, *Reclaiming the Church* (Collins:Fount, 1988), p. 156.

Maintenance Mode	Mission Mode
Teaching and learning the faith	Having a gospel to proclaim
Faithful churchmanship	Being open to the Holy Spirit
Focused on the needs of the church	Focused on the needs of the world
Correct performance of the liturgy	Seeking an experience of God
Performing rites of passage	Nurturing all ages

* * *

To move a church corporately, and to move people individually within the church, from one set of values to another is not a task to be overlooked or underestimated. It is a spiritual renewal which only the Holy Spirit himself can accomplish. It is that very spiritual renewal about which I was writing in the first section of this book. With all its difficulties and traumas, it is not a task which can be avoided or cut short, if we are truly to see the church moving from maintenance to mission.

Sadly, this renewal is often boxed up in the word 'charismatic' and consigned to a place on the shelf next to other parties or traditions within the church. But unless every church of every party and tradition is radically open to the power of the Holy Spirit (which is all that charismatic renewal is about), it will not make that transition from maintenance to mission which so many people, not least in the hierarchy of the church, recognise as so vital and so urgent. As I wrote in *Speak to these Bones*, 'Trying to run a church without the power from on high is like trying to run a car without petrol.'

Even when this renewal of the church has taken place at both the individual and congregational level, there still remain obstacles and constraints in the structures of the church. To those we must now turn.

PART THREE

Obstacles to Renewal

7

Romanticism v. Reality

In 1970 I became the rector of a country parish. It was a village in Lincolnshire, one of the largest and still one of the most rural of the English shires. On my first Christmas Eve I walked down to the little Norman church, with its squat round arches and its old oil lamps. The village blacksmith was tolling the bell, calling the parishioners to the midnight service. The windowsills were decorated with holly and laurel from the manor house across the road. Candles flickered on the altar. We read the ancient story of the Word made flesh, and sang the familiar carols about angels and shepherds, Mary and Joseph, and the babe lying in a manger.

At the end of the service I stood at the old oak door and wished the parishioners a merry Christmas one by one. Then, as I walked back up the hill to the rectory, it started to snow, large, slow flakes settling on the fields and hedgerows. It was magical. At home I climbed the stairs to where my wife and our two-year-old daughter were already in bed and asleep. I crept into our daughter's bedroom and carefully hung her bulging Christmas stocking at the foot of her bed.

The following morning all was white. It was our daughter's first experience of snow. We put on our boots and tramped down to church again for the Christmas morning service, greeting the other worshippers excitedly as we gathered in the church. Christmas Day drinks with the major at the Old Rectory, a blazing log fire, presents round the Christmas tree, turkey and plum pudding: it was pure enchantment.

I remained under the spell of that enchantment for many years, and I can still feel its pull, especially at Christmas. I guess I am not the only one. It is illustrated in thousands of Christmas cards which even the nonreligious send one another, usually adorned with crinolines and stagecoaches. It could be said that the Church of England corporately lives under that same enchantment. But it is Disneyland, a little local theme park we try to maintain, an exercise in nostalgia in which we indulge once a year. The whole of Christmas is just that for most people, and much of the life of the church is the same: fantasyland, a dream of some imagined past.

The reality of my country parish 30 years ago was that fewer and fewer people were coming to church, even at Christmas. The reality today is that the parish is now one of a group. The reality is that many such village churches are virtually bankrupt. The reality is that the vast majority of the villagers go about their daily lives as if the church and the rector did not exist. The reality is that the majority of the young people in the village have never voluntarily entered the church in their lives. The reality is that for most people, yesterday and today, Christmas is not about the birth of Jesus at all, but about food and drink and mountains of debt, and an increase in the rates of divorce and suicide. The reality is that most of what we do in our churches at Christmas is not making contact with the real world at all. The reality is that in ten years' time many of our village churches will be closed.

The communities in which these country churches are set have changed radically. Until the Second World War many country people would not have gone beyond the parish boundary from one week's end to another. All the everyday necessities of life could be found in the parish: home, work, food, school, church and entertainment. An occasional journey to the market town five miles away was as far as many people would go in a year. It is the world of *Cider with Rosie*, but the author, Laurie Lee, chronicles with great insight and precision the way that world ended:

> The brass-lamped motor-car came coughing up the road, followed by the clamorous charabanc; the solid-tyred bus climbed the dusty hills and more people came and went. Chickens and dogs were the early sacrifices, falling demented beneath the wheels. The old folk, too, had strokes and seizures, faced by speeds beyond comprehension. Then scarlet motor-bikes, the size of five-barred gates, began to appear in the village, on which our youths roared like rockets up the two-minute hills, then spent weeks making repairs and adjustments.[1]

The coming of the railways and the invention of the bicycle in the nineteenth century had released the countryman from what had virtually been a prison. The coming of the internal combustion engine, especially since the Second World War, has dissolved almost all the ties which previously bound people and places. Whether we like it or not, we live in the age of the motor car, and the motor car has had a more radical effect on the life of the countryside than anything else since the ground was first ploughed. The nostalgia for the old country church is part of a nostalgia for the old country village.

People who have become rootless pine for an imagined sense of familiarity and belonging in the world. People who are jaded with noise and stress long for the imagined peace of a life spent leaning on a five-barred gate and sucking straw. People who are satiated with possessions and technology dream of an imagined simplicity and self-sufficiency. People sick of street lights and traffic fumes buy a country cottage or a retirement bungalow and try to discover the door to a lost world, where the air is clean and the night sky is full of stars. But the reality of village life is different from the myth.

---

1 Laurie Lee, *Cider with Rosie* (Penguin, 1962), p. 216.

The reality is that today the village is, at the most, one of many different communities to which people belong, communities connected by bus and by car. This is true of everyone in the countryside, not least the young. For children, the most significant community outside the home is school. Playschool and primary school are probably not in the village; secondary school certainly is not. Tertiary education means towns and cities many miles from home. For adults, work is the most significant community outside the home, and only for a very small minority is their work in the same community in which they live. Outside this small minority everyone goes out of the village to work, usually by car. As access to the motor car has become more widespread, village shops have closed. People do their shopping at the supermarket five miles away, by car. Relatives may now live all over the country, or even all over the world, but probably not round the corner in the same village. The golf club, the places to eat out, the entertainment, all mean getting in the car. For many people the only thing they do in the village apart from sleep is watch television.

In every village there is a small group of people whose mission in life is to run the village and do their best to keep it alive. They are public-spirited people who believe in and love the village community. They are the village 'mafia': they run the parish council, the Women's Institute, the village hall or community centre, and probably the parish church as well. They attend and run the coffee mornings, the village fêtes, the jumble sales. More or less successfully, they jolly or bully the rest of the parishioners into joining in with them, but for the most part the lives and hearts of the residents are engaged elsewhere.

Everyone recognises that in cities and suburbs parish boundaries mean little or nothing. In rural areas parishes still seem to be separate entities, because geographically each settlement is still divided from the next by two miles of open fields. But that separateness is a delusion: the motor car has abolished it. The country cousins are even more mobile than their relatives in town. They drive about to their many and varied activities, and they drive their children about, with much less hassle and frustration than their cousins in town, who are struggling with traffic congestion and parking problems. But it is the same way of life.

Everyone now, except the Church of England, has more or less willingly embraced and adjusted to this new way of life. The smaller village schools have closed and the children take the bus together to a larger school in a neighbouring village or country town. Gone are the Victorian schoolrooms with their tortoise stoves, and one or two teachers instilling the three Rs into classes of all ages and all abilities. Now the children are taught in a light, colourful, modern building with facilities for games, science, music and information technology, and a full curriculum differentiated according to every child's age and ability.

Many village shops have closed. Gone are the village bakers and the village butchers, and if a shop remains in the village at all it is a general store combining its role with that of post office and newsagent in order to make ends meet. Many public houses have closed. In a village where perhaps there were once three or four, there is now one, and that serves food to people eating out as much as pints of beer to the locals. Most of the village chapels have closed, as declining and elderly congregations have given up the unequal struggle to pay a minister and keep their own doors open. Only the Church of England has steadfastly stood against the tide of change.

Some people deplore the changes that the motor car has brought: every village school, village shop, village pub or village chapel that closes is bewailed as the passing of an era. It is. But if the old days and old ways of life in the village were so good, why was everyone so eager to climb into the car as soon as it appeared, and drive away from them? The fact is that for most country people the advent of the motor car has opened up a life of infinitely more variety, infinitely more opportunity, and infinitely more stimulation than the old, enclosed world of the village ever offered. The reality of life in the old village, whatever the romantic view, was that it was hard, dull, dark, wet, cold, smelly and short. Without the motor car, modern man and modern woman, seeking to recapture the rural idyll, would quickly find life in the country unbearable and scuttle back to the bright lights of the town as fast as they could. It may not be all gain, but the inhabitants of today's countryside have more opportunities of employment, their children more opportunities of education, all of them more opportunities of enjoyment and leisure, than their forefathers ever dreamed of. No one who has been to Tesco's or Sainsbury's, or one of the other large supermarkets, is ever going back to the village shop except for the things they forgot.

Two factors have driven the changes which the motor car has made possible. The first is that everything can now be done better than it was in the old days. The children get a better education; the supermarkets are a better way to shop; the hospital may be 20 miles away, but it offers better health care. The second factor is money. Village schools closed, usually against local sentiment, because the cost of education for children in small schools was too high. Village shops closed because they could not compete with the supermarkets for either choice or price.

When we turn to the church, however, and to the Church of England in particular, we find a complete lack of vision about any other way of being or doing church than the inherited one, and a stubborn, even heroic, refusal to acknowledge the economic facts of life. The Church of England is in the grip of a nostalgia for the past and an ideology of the parish to such an extent that it looks as if the church will go bankrupt before it lets go of them. Its own nostalgia for a past in which the church counted for more than it does now in people's lives, and people's nostalgia for a past in which the village itself counted for more than it does now in people's lives, have become focused on the parish church, the most conspicuous relic of that long-lost past. But nostalgia is not a sound basis for policy, nor a sound guide to the future. Nostalgia and anxiety are both symptomatic of a lack of faith. It is as if we believe that God cannot live with the motor car, that he cannot cope with the way we live now.

When the economic facts of life finally drag the Church of England out of the Middle Ages, it will be accompanied for many by a sense of failure and despair. Why, however, should the future of the church and its worshippers not be as bright as the future of the schools and their children, or the future of the supermarkets and their shoppers? Of course there are problems with the way we live now, but the clock is not going to start running backwards. If the age of the motor car were ever to come to a sudden and shuddering halt, much more than our ability to drive to church would be affected: our whole way of life would come to an end. Meanwhile, we have to adapt to the twenty-first century as it now is, and as it will evolve from now on. The future can be better than the past, for the church as much as for everyone else.

* * *

In 1999 the parishes of the diocese of Norwich reported their actual Sunday attendances during the month of October. A total of 568 parishes reported. In 318 parishes (56 per cent) average attendance on ordinary Sundays did not reach 20 people, and in 96 of those (17 per cent) average attendance had not even reached double figures. In only 81 churches (14 per cent) were average attendances in excess of 60. Perhaps most significant of all, 253 parishes (45 per cent) reported that during the whole month no one under the age of 16 had attended church at all.

Much clerical time and effort and much diocesan money is absorbed in servicing such small churches and congregations.

But to what end? What purpose is being served for the kingdom of God? How do we justify such expenditure of manpower
and money? Is it a costly exercise in nostalgia? Is the diocese a
sort of hospice for dying churches? It is kind to the terminally
ill to provide a ministry of spiritual encouragement and
comfort – so are we sitting by the bedside of these elderly
churches and holding their hands while they die? Or do we see
ourselves as valiantly holding the fort, with ever-dwindling
troops, in the hope that before the end the cavalry will come
riding over the hill and we shall be saved? If so, how do we
imagine this cavalry, and how do we imagine it will appear?

Let us try to be realistic again. Perhaps there will be some
change in the spiritual climate of the nation which will mean
that people are more open to spiritual things than they appear
to be now. There are signs that such a change is already beginning to take place. Perhaps that means that someday someone
will walk up the path of one of these rural churches looking for
God. If so, will they find him in one of these cold, meagrely
attended services? All things are possible with God, but some
are more likely than others. And if our seeker does have an
experience of God in that service, who is there to take him
aside and explain to him the meaning of the gospel, lead him
to Christ, nurture and disciple him?

Suppose, more plausibly, that someone in the village hears
the gospel from a friend, or has an experience of God elsewhere. She comes to her village church full of her new discov-
ery, eager for another encounter with the living God. What will
she find when she arrives? Any more than a dispirited repeti-
tion of the liturgy? Any more than the fellowship of a few
elderly people whose presence has more to do with habit and
duty than joy and expectation? Will our new Christian not
decide to look elsewhere for the support and encouragement
she certainly needs?

Or again, perhaps a new family moves into the village, with
three or four lively children. They are used to going to church
in a suburban parish with guitars and drums and an imagina-

tive family service. True to their desire to rediscover the values of country life, they turn up at the village church on Sunday morning, only to find themselves sitting through an incomprehensible rigmarole out of a musty Prayer Book and singing four nineteenth-century hymns out of a musty hymnbook. On the way home the children all announce that they are never going to church again if that is what church means here, and the teenager points out that there was no one of her age even in sight. So the parents, who might survive the village church themselves, decide that if their own children are to grow up to love and serve the Lord at all, they must find another church before next week.

We need to examine the concept of 'a viable church'. Viable means 'capable of living, surviving: (of plan or project) of such a kind that it has a prospect of success'.[2] A viable church simply means a church with a future. So what is necessary for a church to be viable? I would suggest that the following is a minimum list of characteristics.

- Real spirituality
- Inspiring worship
- Good music
- Children's work
- Youth work
- Programme for enquirers
- Loving relationships
- Pastoral care
- Cultural relevance
- Adequate finance

• *Real spirituality* If people are looking for anything distinctive in a church, as opposed to any other club, they are looking for some satisfaction of their spiritual longings. They will only find

---

2 *Chambers Twentieth Century Dictionary.*

that if the church is a body of people who themselves have a real relationship with God.

• *Inspiring worship* One of the characteristics of the postmodern world is the desire for more than enlightenment or rational knowledge – the desire for experience. People want to know more than the fact that God exists; they want to know him. They will meet with God in a church service only if their fellow worshippers are seeking more of God for themselves.

• *Good music* Thanks to modern audiovisual technology, music plays a huge part in people's lives today, especially in the lives of the young. People are used to the highest standards, whatever their taste may be. So whatever we sing or play in church in the way of hymns and songs, we must do it well (without falling into the trap of worshipping music instead of God).

• *Children's work* It is a natural and thoroughly scriptural desire of believing parents to want to pass on their knowledge of God and his salvation to their children. Christian parents are therefore looking for a church which will make Christianity attractive and exciting to children. Parents simply cannot afford to stay in a church which is not giving them any help.

• *Youth work* Young people are not usually found in ones; a church will either have lots of young people or none. Perhaps the chief factor in the long, slow decline of the churches has been the disappearance of generation after generation of Sunday school children at the point when they reached puberty. All the comforting assurances about them coming back later have proved false: they went, and most of them went for good.

• *Programme for enquirers* There are so many people today in Western society without even the most basic understanding of the Christian faith that we cannot even think of them coming back: they were never there in the first place. If those people are to find God through Jesus Christ, the local church must provide a way of introducing them to the basic truths and practices of Christianity. It does not have to be Alpha. But is there anything better?

• *Loving relationships* It has been justly said that people may go to a church once for all sorts of reasons, but they will only carry on going if they make friends there. The only new commandment that Jesus gave was that we should love one another (John 15:17). There must be a quality of openness and a genuine welcome for new and perhaps awkward people if the church is to grow.

• *Pastoral care* No one comes to faith, grows in faith and goes on in faith without encountering problems. If these problems are not to prove fatal, the church must have some system of caring for people, keeping in touch with them at more than the superficial level, and providing the ongoing counsel and support that they will need.

• *Cultural relevance* The teaching and life of the church must connect with the daily lives of the people who come, their needs, their aspirations, their difficulties, their hurts. The activities of the church as a body must connect with the wider needs of the community and the world around. A church wrapped up in its own concerns and inner workings only deserves to die.

• *Adequate finance* No church is viable in the long term unless it is financially self-supporting. The more enlightened of the overseas missionaries of the last two centuries realised that their new churches needed to become self-propagating, self-governing and self-financing – the 'three selfs'. In a missionary situation at home, many of our rural churches need to learn the same lessons. At the moment, self-governing they may be; self-propagating and self-financing they are not.

All these ten factors point in a single direction: viability is a function of size. A viable church must contain enough people of all ages. It must contain enough people to supply the various gifts and ministries that the church needs – teachers and preachers, pastors, musicians, children's workers and youth workers. It must contain enough people who are big enough givers to finance the work and the workers. How big, then, must a church be to be viable?

In this context it is worth noticing that in the first three centuries the wisdom of the church was that a body of believers had to include at least 12 fathers of families, before the bishop would recognise them as a separate congregation.[3] When we recall that such a family in the Roman Empire would have included not only wife and children, but also other relatives, servants and slaves, it can be seen that this stipulation must have meant that such a congregation must have numbered at least 60 people of all ages from the start. How such a group was built up in the first place is another story, but the early church clearly recognised that size and the associated financial resources were an essential factor in creating viable churches. By such a standard, out of these 568 parish churches in the diocese of Norwich, only perhaps 80 could be considered viable.

That does not mean that there is no place in the Christian life for smaller groups of believers to gather. It is commonplace to recognise that Christians need to experience God and the fellowship of other believers in groups of three distinct sizes: the cell, the congregation and the celebration. The trouble with too many of our rural churches today is that they should be functioning as cells, but they are trying to function as congregations. It is perfectly possible, given the right conditions, for cells or clusters of cells to grow into new congregations. But it is also only too possible for congregations which are too small or too lacking in spiritual vitality to wither and die.

*　　*　　*

---

3 Edward Schillebeeckx, *Ministry* (SCM, 1981), p. 72: 'Throughout the pre-Nicene church it was held, evidently on the basis of Jewish models, that a community in which at least twelve fathers of families were assembled had the right to a priest or community leader and thus to the eucharist at which he presided.'

It must be possible to perceive in all this the outlines of a strategy both for renewed church growth and for managing a situation of decline. But such a strategy means abandoning our love affair with the past and our nostalgia for the golden age, and taking seriously the fresh imperative of mission and the exciting possibilities of a new age.

8

Ideology v. Pragmatism

The origins of the parish system are obscured in the mists of the Dark Ages and difficult to trace. The most thorough study of the subject that I have discovered is in two short monographs by G.W.O. Addleshaw.[1] Most of what follows is derived from these two articles.

There is an ancient Greek word, *paroikia*, which appears in the New Testament and means 'residence in a foreign land' or 'residence as a stranger'. It passed into Latin as *parochia*, with the meaning of a unit of ecclesiastical administration, or the primary unit of the church's missionary organisation. The *parochia* was the Christian community in a city. Its leader was the bishop. Usually it would consist of a single congregation meeting in a single place. Sometimes, in a larger city, there might be more than one church. In the *parochia* of Rome in AD 300 there were 25 congregations, each served by five or six priests, but only the Bishop of Rome (the Pope) celebrated the mass, which he did in each church in turn. The *parochia* owned all church property, and out of the people's offerings the bishop paid the clergy.

---

1 G. W. O. Addleshaw, *The Beginnings of the Parochial System* and *The Development of the Parochial System from Charlemagne to Urban II* (St Anthony's Hall, York, 1953 and 1954).

Early Christianity spread from the towns and cities out into the countryside as bishops went out preaching from village to village, and the gospel was carried by less formal means and personal contacts. As groups of believers were formed and started meeting together, churches were built in the larger villages or at strategic places on the main roads. No attempt was made, however, to divide the area up into separate geographical portions, nor to build churches in every centre of population. In missionary mode, the converts came first, followed by whatever buildings were necessary for their use and worship.

At the end of the fourth century in Tours in northern France, Martin, who became bishop in AD 372, began the evangelisation of the surrounding countryside. During the 25 years of his episcopate he planted and built six churches to serve the rural areas. In the following century another 16 were added.

Canon laws of the church in Gaul in the sixth century distinguished three different kinds of church. There were the city churches, where the bishops resided, usually living in community with their clergy; the country churches, which were also served by several priests and deacons living in community; and private chapels on some of the great estates, ministering to the spiritual needs of the households of the noblemen. The country churches no less than the city ones were still mission stations, with the responsibility of evangelising and planting yet more congregations. The private chapels, on the other hand, built by great landowners within their castles or villas, sometimes outside the jurisdiction of the local bishop and to which the nobleman usually appointed his own priest, did not have the same missionary mandate or motivation: they served only the entourage of the magnate. It is from these private chapels rather than the diocesan mission stations that parish churches are descended.

In England, Augustine, who landed in AD 597, established a number of mission centres in the south, each under the leadership of a bishop. It was a later Archbishop of Canterbury, Theodore, who divided England up into geographical dioceses.

Within each diocese the church's work was carried on from mission stations which were called 'minsters', a word preserved today in certain English place names. Each minster was staffed by a number of clergy living a communal life, often based on a monastery or convent. In a larger minster, like the one at Canterbury in 805, there were eight priests as well as other minor clergy; in a smaller one there were perhaps just two or three priests. From the minster the clergy would sally out into the surrounding villages to preach, baptise and say mass, often in the open air, under a cross set up for the purpose. English minsters were the equivalent of Martin's country churches in France. In the diocese of Canterbury in the eighth century there were seven such mission stations.

As time went by, more and more village churches were built, sometimes at the initiative of the bishop, sometimes at the behest of a Saxon thane or earl, sometimes by a monastery to serve a village on monastic lands. As early as 734 the Venerable Bede wrote to Egbert, Bishop of York, encouraging him to provide a more regular ministry of word and sacrament to village people, and resident priests to care for their souls. Across the channel in France, at about the same time, the reign of Charlemagne saw the beginnings of a movement for the establishment of a church and a priest in every village. We are approaching the concept of the parish system as we know it today. By the end of the eleventh century, most of Europe north of the Alps was organised on this basis.

This 'second generation' of country churches was largely founded by local landowners, ecclesiastical or lay. By this time the feudal system was fully established throughout northern Europe, and the church and its life increasingly became an appendage of the feudal manor. The village church would be built at the initiative and expense of the lord of the manor, the work done by the craftsmen of the manor. The lord of the manor then assumed for himself the right to appoint a priest to serve his church, and he set aside land as an endowment, for the upkeep of the church and the support of the priest.

A crucial piece of legislation was enacted in France in 765 by Pepin the Short, and in England some 200 years later by the Saxon King Edmund. The agricultural tithe, a land rent payable to the church in cash or in kind, was made compulsory. Up to this time offerings to the church of whatever kind had remained a matter of free will. Now the local church and the local priest were legally entitled to tithe rents from all the lands in the parish. At that moment parish boundaries became important, especially to the clergy! The ecclesiastical parish was the area of land from which the parish priest received the tithes.

The parish churches thus established were under a dual authority, that of the lord of the manor and that of the bishop. Canon lawyers of the eleventh century codified the delicate relationships between bishop, patron and parish priest – laws which were first enacted by Ethelred the Unready and King Canute, but which have governed the parish churches of England more or less unchanged down to the present day. The patron has the right of presentation to the parish; the parish priest so presented has a 'freehold' and cannot be evicted; the priest is under the authority of the bishop in his ecclesiastical functions; parishioners must take their share in the upkeep of the fabric of their parish church.

The Domesday Book reveals the prevalence of the parish system by 1086. As the settlements and manors of England are counted and catalogued, there is a frequent note concluding, 'There is a church and a priest.' The Domesday Book still uses the term 'old minster' to denote the survival of the Anglo-Saxon mission centres. In the south and east the parish system is comprehensively established: in Norfolk there are 217 parish churches recorded. In the north and west of England, however, there are many more signs of the minster system remaining even after the Norman Conquest. The Domesday Book shows us a particular stage, a late stage, in the process by which the primary unit of church life in England changed from being the minster to being the parish church.

This is precisely the point at which the church changed out of missionary mode and into maintenance mode. It is a process which extended over several hundred years, but the change from minster to parish is the change from mission to maintenance. The logic of that for our present situation should not need spelling out: if we are to move back from maintenance to mission, we have to move back from the parish system to some sort of modern 'minster' system. In the meantime, however, the parish system has become not just a practice but an ideology.

*   *   *

The idea of the parish system is the younger brother of the idea of Christendom. In the age of Christendom the church ceased to be understood as a voluntary association of people who had decided to follow Jesus. The church reverted to an Old Testament model of the nation as a holy people. The New Testament had turned the Old Testament concept upside down, and declared that the people of God were a holy nation. But, without any scriptural justification, the idea subtly turned itself inside out again. Instead of the church being a Christian island in a sea of paganism, the new Jerusalem was deemed to have come down from heaven already, and there was no more sea. It cannot be said too clearly or too strongly that in Christian terms the communal model of the church, as opposed to the associational model, is just plain heresy.

The corollary of the idea of Christendom is that the church's responsibility is to provide pastoral care for everyone in the nation and to minister to everyone the rites of the church. The parish system is a neat way of doing that. Under the parish system the whole country is divided up into a sort of grid: each unit in the grid is a parish; each parish has a parish church; each parish church is served by a parish priest; each parish priest is maintained by an endowment; all the people living within the parish boundaries are the parishioners. All the parishioners are supposed to resort to their parish church to do their spiritual duties, and each parishioner has a right to the ministrations of the parish priest. Each parishioner has a share in the responsibility for the upkeep of the parish church, and a corresponding voice in its affairs. In the countryside the parochial grid usually bore some reasonable relationship to the natural communities within it; in the towns and cities the grid was always arbitrary. The ideology demanded that everyone should be covered by the parish system – and everyone was, and everyone still is.

Like all bureaucratic systems, the parish system always worked better on paper than on the ground, better in the mind than in practice. Throughout the Middle Ages the problem was the ignorance of the parish clergy: the blind leading the blind and the dumb teaching the dumb. In the eighteenth century, after the fierce intolerances of the Reformation, the clergy became lethargic. In Jane Austen's *Mansfield Park*, Mary Crawford exclaims, 'A clergyman has nothing to do but to be slovenly and selfish, read the newspaper, watch the weather, and quarrel with his wife. His curate does all the work, and the business of his own life is to dine.' To read the contemporary diaries of Parson Woodforde is to realise how near to the truth that waspish remark came. The needs of these gentleman-parsons to support the manner of life to which they were accustomed, and the meanness of the endowments which went with many of their country livings, gave rise to widespread pluralism and nonresidence.

If there was ever a golden age of the parish system, it was the century from 1850 to 1950. In that period, perhaps as at no other time before or since, the vision was realised: each village with its own church and its own priest, and, given the vagaries of human nature, priests who were seriously dedicated to their calling and professionally equipped for it. Nonetheless, even this apparently idyllic state of affairs bred boredom and eccentricity among the clergy. Many of these serious and professional country clergy served less than 200 parishioners, and simply did not have enough to do except play tennis with their daughters and take tea on the lawn. A friend of the Russell family who had recently taken a country parish in Lincolnshire in the 1870s wrote to a relative, 'My clerical neighbours are exhaustively divisible into three classes – those who have gone out of their minds, those who are going out of them, and those who have no minds to go out of.'

Whatever the merits or faults of the parish system in previous generations, in the last 50 years this venerable system has quietly and unobtrusively collapsed. Step by step the Church of England has dismantled the structure, not for ideological but for purely pragmatic reasons.

The first step, in the years after the Second World War, was the deliberate creation in the countryside of groups of parishes staffed by teams of clergy. The initial experiment was made at South Ormsby in Lincolnshire, an experiment recorded by the first rector, Arthur Smith.[2] The pattern was copied widely, especially in the dioceses of Lincoln and Norwich. Anything up to ten or more small country parishes were grouped together for pastoral purposes under a team of, initially, three or four ministers. It was an arrangement which the motor car made possible: the clergy began to drive from church to church and village to village to perform their duties. It is instructive that the advantages Arthur Smith claimed for the new system accrued almost exclusively to the clergy. It was an escape from rural isolation, it afforded them the fellowship of other professionals, and it enabled curates to be trained in a rural environment. The lay people were left comparatively undisturbed in their villages, but the first brick had been removed from the parish system: the ideal of matching each parish and church with its own parish priest was abandoned. Ideology was giving way to pragmatism.

---

2 A. C. Smith, *The South Ormsby Experiment* (SPCK, 1960).

This process was vastly accelerated in the 1960s and 1970s by two further developments. The first was a report entitled *The Deployment and Payment of the Clergy*, produced by Leslie Paul in 1964, which led to a deliberate redeployment of the Anglican clergy in favour of the urban areas. In terms of the general movement of the population and the growth of the cities over the previous 200 years, the case for this was unanswerable and the change long overdue. The second development, unforeseen in 1964, was a catastrophic decline in the number of ordained people. The number of stipendiary clergy in the Church of England dropped from 15,488 in 1961 to 10,992 in 1981. This, coupled with the policy of redeployment, meant that rural areas simply emptied of stipendiary priests in less than a generation. In one typical rural deanery the number of incumbents in office in 27 country parishes dropped from 15 to 5 in 30 years. The multi-parish benefices which had been staffed by three or four ministers in the 1950s and 1960s became multi-parish benefices staffed by a single priest in the 1990s. No longer are large pluralities and nonresidence scandalous, as they were in the eighteenth century; today they are the norm. The formula of one parish, one church, one priest has broken down completely.

Other inroads just as fatal to the old parish system, though perhaps less obvious, have also been made in the name of common sense. Over the last 40 years there has been a massive movement of centralisation and bureaucratisation in the Church of England. By stages, ownership of and responsibility for the dilapidations of parsonage houses, and ownership and management of endowments and glebe, all the benefice property, has passed into diocesan hands. Without doubt this has led to administration which has been more consistent and effective. Moreover, late-twentieth-century clergy refused to tolerate the baseless variations in income between one parish and the next, as their predecessors did. So, alongside the centralised management of assets has come the centralised payment of stipends and pensions, and with that the centralised deployment of clerical manpower.

Each reform as it has come along has been manifestly fair, rational and necessary. But each reform has removed yet more bricks from the edifice of the parish system. Pragmatism has triumphed. In spite of these changes, however, the legal framework of the parish system still remains largely intact, and the ideology of the parish system still exerts a fatal fascination over both clergy and people alike.

* * *

In *Church and Religion in Rural England*, Davies and others wrote in 1991,

> It is easy to debate the nature of Anglicanism in terms of a three-fold order of ministry set amidst the Prayer Book, the place of Reason in interpreting scripture, and Church Tradition. A better way of characterising the Church, however, might be in its parish organisation and ethos. The Parochial System constitutes the Church of England.[3]

From any theological standpoint that is a breathtaking statement. From the standpoint of other Anglican churches throughout the world, in the USA for example, which operate perfectly well without our parish system, it sounds, well, parochial. But it does say something only too true about the stranglehold which the ideology of the parish system has on the Church of England. The parish system has become an idol. The Church of England, that most undogmatic of churches ever since the Reformation, can be elastic about the virgin birth or the bodily resurrection of Jesus, about the ordination of women

---

3 D. Davies, *Church and Religion in Rural England* (T. & T. Clark, 1991), p. 26.

or the practice of homosexuality, but the parish system is unquestioned and unquestionable: it defines our identity. The ideology of the parish system has become a major obstacle to renewal, especially the renewal of the church for mission.

The parish system grew up with the church in maintenance or Christendom mode. Mission is simply not in its DNA. The parish system obscures for everyone, in the church and outside it, the fact that some people in our society are Christians and others are not, and that to be a Christian in adult life requires a conscious choice and decision. No one is a Christian by default. Of course, no one is in a position to judge finally who is saved and who is not: God alone is the judge, and that judgement is the last. But something like the parish system, which obscures the distinction between being saved and being lost and blurs the necessity for every human being to choose between life and death, is a positive hindrance to mission.

The parish system is deceptive in a second way: the existence of a church in every parish, in the sense of a church building, leads us to suppose that there is a church in every parish, in the sense of a viable congregation of faithful people. We therefore continue to feel obliged to provide a ministry in every church, even though that means in practice that we are often serving buildings rather than people. The life of the church and the pattern of its ministry are dictated by the existence and location of church buildings, rather than by the needs of people or by an effective strategy of mission. The efforts of the church are directed towards keeping up buildings and keeping up a semblance of worship within them. As a strategy for mission, that has been failing for at least 100 years.

The parish system is also exclusive. The theory, of course, is that it is inclusive of everyone within the parish. The fact is, however, that a great many people within the parish do not want to be included and strenuously resist all attempts to include them. The opposite effect is that everyone outside the parish is, both in theory and often in practice, excluded. The parish system brings with it an eleventh commandment, 'Thou shall worship in thine own parish church and in no other.' In most country villages today, probably as many people get in their cars and drive out of the parish to go to church as get in their cars and drive to their own parish church. But the Anglicans at least do so with a sense of guilt, and anyone driving into a country parish to go to church is going to feel more or less of an intruder, however long they continue to come.

*   *   *

The parish system is not an effective structure for mission in the twenty-first century. People do not belong to a single community, but to many different communities; they have networks of friends and relationships formed in many different ways. If the church draws a line round the local community and says that only people on the right side of that line belong to that church (which the parish system does), then the biggest part of most people's lives is rendered inoperative for the purposes of church-based evangelism.

The church needs to re-establish itself as a distinct and distinctive community within society, which is joined by voluntary association. There is no other and no better reason for this than that the New Testament church founded by Jesus Christ can never be anything else. The church must break its bondage to buildings if it is to be free to develop a strategy of mission. Finally, in the world today there is a horizon to the contacts and relationships of everyday life, but, thanks to the motor car, it is a much wider horizon than the parish boundary. The parish system belonged to the age of Christendom, which is long past. It was never a missionary system. If the church is ever to move from maintenance to mission, the legal framework of the parish system and the ideology to which it gave rise must be buried. The future is not parish-shaped but network-shaped.

9

Conservation v. Change

Each historic renewal of the church has made an impact on the church buildings. At the Reformation in the sixteenth century the altars were removed from the east end and brought down into the nave of the church. The carved figures of Christ on the cross, Mary and John were removed from the rood screen. Medieval wall paintings, often featuring the Day of Doom, were whitewashed and overlaid with scriptural texts. During the English Civil War in the seventeenth century many images of the saints in stone and stained glass were smashed or defaced. The medieval church buildings with their architectural logic and their visual aids for an illiterate population were ruthlessly hacked about to express the primacy of the word, the priesthood of all believers and a fierce Puritanism.

In the nineteenth century a reaction against the ugliness of industrialisation and the culture of muck and brass produced Victorian romanticism – of nature on the one hand, and of the Middle Ages on the other. While Sir Walter Scott and Alfred Lord Tennyson romanticised about medieval knights and the death of Arthur, Newman, Pusey and Keble romanticised about the medieval church. The so-called Oxford Movement was a romantic attempt to recreate that medieval church. Listen to Canon Henry Scott Holland rhapsodising to the daughter of the prime minister, William Gladstone, about the appointment of a notable Anglo-Catholic, Edward King, to the bishopric of Lincoln:

> Bless you for the Surprise and Delight of King. A St Francis de Sales at Lincoln. A joy like an old Spring, if you can fancy Spring grown old ... It is lovely as a dream, King moving through the dim Fens on a slow-pacing cob – blessing kneeling peasants. He will move as a benediction.[1]

Ineffably silly as that is, this romantic revival had a profound effect on our churches. The tables went back to the east end and were renamed 'altars'. A choir was reinstalled in the chancel, robed and singing the services in place of the medieval monks. Vestments and candles not seen in English churches for 300 years reappeared. Many a stained-glass window was commissioned to replace the ones that Cromwell had destroyed. The many new churches that were built in the rapidly expanding industrial towns deliberately imitated the vaulting arches and pillared aisles of medieval cathedrals. Brick might have replaced stone, but the design and the shapes were still Gothic. While the theological and liturgical revival is known as the Oxford Movement, this architectural revival owes more to the Cambridge Camden Society. But while the Oxford Movement had a limited and controversial impact, this Cambridge Movement influenced and affected the fabric and furnishings of practically every church building in England.

Today the church is in the midst of another reformation and revival. Like its predecessors, this revival is leading to a desire to renew the physical surroundings of the church's work and worship. In the story of our own parish church, it was at this point that the irresistible force of spiritual renewal met an immovable object: the rock of modern conservationism.

---

1 Quoted by J. A. Newton in 'Bishop, King and Nonconformity', *Theology* (SPCK, 1971).

* * *

Faced with a legal dogfight over the removal of our pews, we simply baled out of the parish church, leaving it to fly on with all its seats intact but rather fewer passengers on board. The full consequences of this course of action we did not foresee, and perhaps could not have foreseen, at the time. But jump we did, and at that moment we escaped from much more than a few old pews: we escaped from the whole snare of conservationism. With one bound, Jack was free.

The people of God in the Church of England, and perhaps in other churches too, are in slavery today. Never mind that for many this is a voluntary slavery, it is still slavery. We are in slavery to the conservationists. The conservationists rule over us through a multitude of official bodies and so-called 'amenity societies' – English Heritage, the Council for the Care of Churches, diocesan advisory committees, consistory courts, the Society for the Protection of Ancient Buildings, the Georgian Group, the Victorian Society, even the Twentieth Century Society. These bodies often pose as friends of the people of God, but they are in reality our taskmasters. Without us the conservationists would not be able to carry on the great works with which they are engaged: the preservation of the national heritage of ancient buildings, in particular our churches and cathedrals. In each city and parish they have a band of more or less willing slaves who do the work for them. It is an army which toils ceaselessly, year in and year out, holding fêtes and jumble sales to raise money for the task of conservation. But should the people of God have the temerity to want to change something in these buildings for which they slave, to remove a pew or install a kitchen, they are likely to feel the crack of the taskmasters' whip across their backs. The people of God must remember their place and their masters.

The church itself colludes in this slavery, and even supplies foremen for the job. Every year in each archdeaconry in the land there is a great gathering of the clergy and leading laity from every church and parish, hundreds of men and an increasing number of women, representing the whole people of God. And what is the subject for this great meeting, or the text for the sermon to this great assembly? Is it the people's desire to deepen their love-relationship with God, as in Matthew 22:37? Is it the Great Commission that Christ has given us for our parishes, in Matthew 28:19? Is it how we are to do the works which Jesus did, as in John 14:12? Is it imaginative ideas for works of mercy appropriate to our own generation, as in Matthew 25:35–37? On the contrary, if there is a text at all it is usually a pretext, and the subject matter is actually the gutters and downspouts, and the need to insure and secure the church's antique furniture and silver plate.

Archdeacons everywhere will insist that this is wilfully to misunderstand the purpose of these services, which are for the admission of churchwardens. And perhaps that is so. But the question still remains: why is this Festival of Gutters and Downspouts the one occasion in the year for which the hierarchy think it worth summoning together all the clergy and churchwardens of the diocese, and the one occasion for which all the clergy and churchwardens actually turn out? Indeed, we fight not against flesh and blood, but against principalities and powers, and spiritual hosts of wickedness in heavenly places. One of the great principalities of our generation is the culture of conservation. We are a society so insecure in the midst of change that every stick and stone from the past must be preserved at all costs. No expenditure of money is too great to preserve and restore a medieval wall painting or a prehistoric henge. We prefer the past to the future.

The experience of many other churches in England has been similar to ours. In Wells-next-the-Sea, a small seaside town, the rector and churchwardens, with the support of the church council, proposed to remove five rows of pews, install a small kitchen and move the font, in order to open up some space at the back of the church for social activities. They were taken to court by 49 people who opposed the scheme, of whom just eight were enrolled as worshipping members of the church. In addition the town council passed a resolution stating, 'We wish the interior of St Nicholas's church to be kept in exactly the same condition as it now is.'

In court the case for change was substantially defeated: no kitchen was allowed, the font had to stay where it was, and just three rows of pews could be moved, but not sold. The reasons why the judge decided in this case as he did are important, because of the light they shed on the obstacles to change.

First, the case for change, the judge said, was simply not presented in a way which could convince him: little evidence was presented to support the need for change. The arguing of the case had fallen to a churchwarden with no experience of the law and little understanding of the requirements of the court. But professional legal representation would have been very expensive. As it was, the whole exercise cost the church council £4,000; the services of a barrister would have multiplied that figure several times over. To effect even minor changes to an historic building can involve financial costs which a small or elderly congregation simply cannot afford – costs out of all proportion to the cost of the actual work.

Second, the law itself favours the status quo. A definitive legal judgement in the nineteenth century states, 'The burden of proof does properly devolve upon those who propose a change.'[2] In a more recent judgement, this principle was refined into three questions which have to be asked in all such cases:

1. Have the petitioners proved a necessity for some or all of the proposed works, either because they are necessary or for the pastoral wellbeing of the church or for some other compelling reason?

---

2 Lord Penzance in Peak v. Trower, 1881.

2. Will some or all of the works adversely affect the character of the church as a building of special architectural and historic interest?
3. If the answer to (2) is yes, then is the necessity proved by the petitioners such that in the exercise of the court's discretion a faculty should be granted for some or all of the works?[3]

It is always going to be difficult to prove the pastoral necessity of, for example, removing pews, when all the opponents have to do is say, 'We like it the way it is.' And even when a necessity is 'proved', that will not automatically override other considerations relating to architectural and historical interest.

Third, anyone can object. Any person resident in the parish is regarded as an interested party, whether or not such a person is in any way active in the life of the church or even a Christian. The town council has a right to be heard. Indeed, it appears from another decision of Lord Penzance that not only the living have a right to be heard, but even the dead and the yet unborn: 'The sacred edifice belongs not to any one generation, nor are its interests and conditions the exclusive care of those who inhabit the parish at any one period of time.'[4]

All this, of course, is consistent with the theology and polity of Christendom. If every inhabitant of the parish is a member of the church, then every inhabitant past, present and to come has a right to a say in what goes on. Our own proposal to remove pews provoked objections from parishioners who rarely, if ever, came to church, from people who had been married in the church years before, and from people whose relatives were buried in the churchyard. The voices of those who worship in and use the church week in, week out can easily be drowned out in the hubbub of dissent.

Thus there are three strong reasons which militate against

---

3 Chancellor Sheila Cameron QC, in re. St Helen's, Bishopsgate, 1993.
4 Nicholls v. Briscoe, 1892.

the renewal of the physical structures: first, the sheer weight and expense of the processes involved; second, the presumption of the law in favour of conservation; third, the involvement of people outside the worshipping congregation. If the church building is seen as a facility for the life and worship of the congregation, there is no justification for any of these three factors. If, on the other hand, the church building is seen as an item in the architectural and historical heritage of the nation, the needs and desires of the worshipping congregation are only one factor among many which have to be taken into account. Every congregation worshipping in a building of architectural or historical interest therefore lives with at least a potential conflict of values – between the values of the kingdom of God and the values of conservation.

It is possible that these two sets of values can be reconciled. Richard Giles has written an excellent and stimulating book called *Repitching the Tent*.[5] In it he discusses the whole process of designing or redesigning a church building as a home or house for a church family with a modern understanding of worship and mission. His survey examines many examples in Britain, continental Europe and the United States, Anglican and Roman Catholic. He cites many projects which have been successfully carried out in buildings both new and old, with delightful and inspiring results. Many of these examples, well photographed and illustrated, demonstrate how it is possible to blend the new and the old together, to adapt older buildings to new liturgical and social requirements. Certainly anyone embarking on such an exercise could not do better than to start by studying Richard Giles's book.

In the end, however, two things need to be said about this approach. First, given the three factors militating against change set out above, success still cannot be guaranteed. Second, why bother in the first place?

---

5 Richard Giles, *Repitching the Tent* (Canterbury Press, 1995).

*   *   *

To do Giles justice, he does suggest that a church should begin by asking itself two radical questions: does it need to own a building at all, and, if so, does it need the building it has inherited from previous generations? Having asked these questions, however, Giles does not pause to consider the monumental consequences of an Anglican parish church saying 'no' to either. Rather, he continues by looking with great imagination at the issues involved in reordering the old place after all. Given our own history, I believe that we need to take a much harder look, especially in many of our country parishes, at the more radical options, even though our country parishes may be the very hardest places in which to embrace radical answers.

We should not despair, however. In 1967 the then Bishop of Norwich, Lancelot Fleming, decided to grasp the nettle of the city churches. At that time there were still no less than 30 medieval churches in use in the city centre. Like London, Bristol and York, Norwich had inherited a host of historic churches, by 1967 out of all proportion to the number of people who actually worshipped or even lived there. Drastic action was needed. As a result of the work of the Brooke Commission, no less than 21 churches were made redundant, vested in the city council, and converted for the most part to other uses. These other uses ranged from an antiques centre and a snack bar to a puppet theatre. If such a radical approach was possible in the city, why not in the countryside?

Richard Giles himself suggests that any plan to rebuild or reorder a church needs to start with what he calls a 'strategic development plan'. This in turn needs to grow out of a mission statement. In other words, questions of buildings and furniture ought to be subsidiary to an understanding of the church as a community called by God for a specific purpose. The articulation of a church's understanding of that purpose is its mission statement, and its strategic development plan is its own attempt to work out how to put that purpose into practice. One aspect of the strategic development plan should be to identify what buildings or premises the church needs to facilitate its mission. This should result in a specification, the sort of thing to which an architect or designer could be instructed to work.

My guess is that, if every church were to take such an approach as this to its buildings and facilities, in nine cases out of ten the conclusion of the exercise could only be that the last thing it wants or needs is what it has got. The trouble is that almost nobody starts with this approach (perhaps for fear of the consequences), but almost everybody starts by taking for granted what they have got, and simply asking how they can make the best of a more or less bad job.

In our case it was, you could say, by accident that we found ourselves in a position where we had to start from scratch and adopt the approach recommended by Richard Giles. We found ourselves with the opportunity to design a new worship centre, purpose-built for the twenty-first century. We drew up a specification, free of any responsibility for maintaining or adapting an ancient monument. We could ask ourselves the radical question, 'What do we really need?' Set out below is our answer, which came out of our own understanding of the church's mission and our own situation.

SPECIFICATION FOR NEW WORSHIP CENTRE

We require:

1. A worship area to seat 250 people, with a low platform in the centre of one wall for an altar-table, lectern, etc., with space to one side for the worship band and to the other for dance/drama ministry. There must be enough height above the platform on the wall for the projection of words on an OHP. Special attention needs to be given to the needs of lighting and ventilation. A baptismal pool as an integral

part, and perhaps a feature, of the worship area should be included.

2. An entrance lobby which is welcoming, with adequate provision for hanging coats.

3. Four subsidiary meeting rooms, each sufficient for 15 or 20 people, with provision for at least two of these rooms to be joined, so as to provide a place for 40 people to meet. One of these rooms should be a dedicated space for young people.

4. Toilets pro rata, including statutory provision for the disabled, and at least one place for nappy changing.

5. A vestry room, which can double as a crèche during services with room for five mothers and toddlers, with access both to the worship area and to the toilets without re-entering the worship area.

6. An office, approx. 30 square metres.

7. Kitchens, conforming to public health and safety regulations, with facilities for providing both hot and cold food and drinks.

8. Car parking pro rata for 250 people.

The building should form a pleasant and attractive environment, both inside and out, so that both passers-by and those entering the building should sense something of the joy and beauty of the Lord from the appearance of the place. We want a building that is simple, friendly, and practical, but which also pleases the eye and the senses, and provides a gracious environment for the Lord's work.

Had we begun with such a specification some years before, we would probably never even have contemplated the removal of the pews in the parish church. It would have been clear from the outset that there was no way in which this Grade 1 listed building could be adapted inside and out to fulfil these requirements. It had not been designed to do so in the first place, and to try now to wrench it into such a form would simply have violated its medieval character. Our exodus from the parish church spared both of us a hideous compromise. The majority of our historic church buildings are never going to fulfil the needs of a twenty-first-century congregation, at least if that congregation's calling is seen in terms of mission rather than maintenance.

At this point, however, the vicious circle begins to close, for many a congregation, especially a rural one, actually sees itself as the village committee for the maintenance of the church building. Many a church council agenda is dominated almost exclusively by questions relating to the fabric and furnishings of the church, and if the vicar insists that the members consider the plight of the church in China or the admission of children to Holy Communion, there is an almost audible sigh of relief when they can get back to discussing the colour of the new carpet for the vestry or who is to organise the cake stall at the church fête. When we led the charismatic congregation out of the parish church and into the village community centre, the chief anxiety we left behind was, 'Who is going to maintain the old building now?'

Jesus remarked that the children of the world are much smarter in their own way than the children of light (Luke 16:8). When it comes to buildings, that is certainly true. One of the great commercial success stories of twentieth-century Britain has been the supermarket chain Tesco's. In the course of 100 years Tesco's has reinvented itself no less than four or five times. Starting on a barrow in London's East End, Jack Cohen bought groceries in bulk and sold them cheap. Between the wars he noticed the explosive growth of the new suburbs, each with its new parade of shops. So Tesco's opened shops, using the same formula, buying in bulk and selling cheap. In the 1950s and 1960s a new way of shopping emerged: out went the long counters, and in came the self-service shelves and the checkouts. In the 1970s the new supermarkets moved out of the high street altogether, in search of more floor space and easier car parking. In the 1980s and 1990s Tesco's began to aim for quality as well as quantity. At each turn the directors saw the way the world was going and moved fast to go with it. So Tesco's prospered and grew throughout the twentieth century.

Each move involved a radical change to the buildings and premises that the firm required to carry on its business. One after another, wheelbarrows, shops, and the high street itself, were abandoned. In business there is no room for sentimentality. Another supermarket chain built a new branch in the 1970s to serve a new housing estate on the edge of a large city. A generation later a bypass was built for the city just beyond the housing estate. A retail park was planned beside the motorway junction, and the supermarket promptly abandoned its premises in the heart of the housing estate in order to rebuild even bigger a mile away on the retail park.

By comparison with Tesco's, the Church of England has failed to reinvent the way it does business even once in 1,000 years. In the age of the supermarket the church is still trying to sell its wares from a wheelbarrow. Can anyone be surprised that, unlike Tesco's, in the twentieth century the Church of England failed and declined? If the comparison with Tesco's has anything to teach us, it is that the children of light are over-attached to their wheelbarrows.

At this point many people will object that church buildings are not the same as supermarkets, not mere facilities from which to conduct a business; they are houses of God, holy places, which it is sacrilege to abandon, or perhaps even to change. Here we stumble across yet another way in which the church has reverted from a New Testament understanding to an Old Testament understanding of itself as the people of God.

In the Old Testament, God chose to put his name in a certain place. At first that place was a moving tent, later it became a fixed temple. As part of his old covenant with the people of Israel, God's presence was particularly found in Jerusalem, in Solomon's temple, and in the Holy of Holies. Although temples came and went, this dispensation lasted until the time of Jesus. Then it changed.

To the great perplexity and consternation of his contemporaries, Jesus spoke of the demolition of the temple and its replacement with the temple of his body (John 2:19–21). The flesh of Jesus was now the tent in which the presence of God dwelled among men. When the body of Jesus was taken up into heaven, the Holy Spirit came to dwell in the believers, making them God's temple (1 Corinthians 3:16–17). The latest temple in Jerusalem, built by King Herod over 46 years, was now redundant; the glory of God had departed and dwelled elsewhere. So it should have been no surprise, and it was no grief to the Christians, when, courtesy of the Romans, the temple was demolished in AD 70, never to be rebuilt. God, at least, does not seem to be sentimental about buildings.

For the better part of 300 years the church existed without buildings at all. The church met in people's houses, in times of persecution underground in the catacombs. Even if a room in a Roman villa was set aside for the church's use, as appears to have been the case at Lullingstone in Kent, that room was a meeting room and not a temple. As late as the third century, Minicius Felix was still able to proclaim, 'We have no temples; we have no altars,' for, as Richard Giles says, 'The Old Covenant had not yet begun to wrap its tentacles around the youthful Church.'

After the conversion of Constantine, however, that is exactly what did happen. The church began to revert to an Old Testament understanding of God and his dwelling places. The temple of Jerusalem was reared up again in every town and hamlet; the theology of the living stones (1 Peter 2:4–5) was replaced again by the theology of the holy place. But God will simply not agree with this. It will not do for the Christian church to replace a New Testament understanding of itself with an Old Testament one, or even to hold the two together alongside one another. Even in the Old Testament the temple became a sort of idol from which the people of God had to be separated (Jeremiah 7:1–15). How much more under the new covenant must the children of God keep themselves from the idolatry of buildings.

Jesus did not say to his disciples, 'Go into all the world and act as custodians of the world's architectural and historical heritage.' It is not that there is anything morally wrong with such works of preservation, but the followers of Jesus have more important fish to fry – or fish to catch. When those first disciples began to wax lyrical about the beauty of stones and the magnificence of buildings, Jesus cut them off sharply and began to teach them about more ultimate things. 'Do you see all these great buildings?' he said. 'Not one stone here will be left on another; every one will be thrown down' (Mark 13:1–2).

Our Norman abbeys and Gothic cathedrals are indeed surpassingly beautiful. No doubt Herod's temple was too. Such buildings stand among the very highest achievements of human art and imagination. Nevertheless, the salvation of souls, the gathering in of a harvest for eternal life, is infinitely more important. In human terms these ancient monuments have outlasted the lifespan of many generations. The philosopher G. E. Moore is said to have passed the Royal Hospital in Chelsea during the Second World War shortly after a bomb had fallen nearby, killing a number of people. 'Thank God,' Moore said, 'the Royal Hospital was spared. People are easily replaced; Wren's masterpiece could never be replaced.' From the perspective of eternity, however, such relative values look very different. Long after the Royal Hospital and all our cathedrals and parish churches have crumbled to dust, those whose names are written in the Lamb's book of life will be walking or dancing on the streets that are golden, and those outside will be lamenting their loss.

It is true that certain buildings or places retain an aura from what has happened in them in the past, both for good and for ill. T. S. Eliot wrote about the chapel in the village of Little Gidding, 'You are here to kneel / Where prayer has been valid.'[6] Many people, visitors and tourists, wander round our

---

6 T. S. Eliot, *Four Quartets*, 'Little Gidding', I, lines 47–48 (Faber and Faber, 1969).

ancient churches and cathedrals, not just to admire the architecture but also to taste the atmosphere of places where prayer has been valid. But yet, what such people need more is to discover places where prayer is valid today and gives hope for tomorrow. Spiritual nostalgia is no more edifying than social nostalgia; old buildings on their own convey no more than that.

*　　*　　*

When all is said and done, our old churches convey a very ambiguous message to the outside world. We would like to think that they speak to the world of a God who is faithful and unchanging through the years, and to some of us inside the church that is what they do say. But the stones themselves say nothing. They do not speak at all, and people cannot call on him in whom they have not believed, and they cannot believe in him of whom they have never heard. It is not stones that people need, but preachers. And the ancient stones may well speak a very different message from the one we want people to hear: a message that the church belongs to the past, is unable to adapt or change, and is therefore irrelevant to people in the present.

The fact is that the mission of the church is not to be a conservation society, but to be an agent of the kingdom of God. As it stands, the strategy of the church is controlled, or at the very least hampered, by its buildings. That is nonsense. When our buildings are not serving and helping to forward the mission strategy of the church, it is time to lock the door and post the keys to English Heritage.

PART FOUR

New Structures

10

Mission Structures

New structures mean new churches outside the parish system, or a radical reform of the parish system, or both. They also mean new buildings or facilities for the work and worship of the church, remembering always that the motive and justification for these changes is the imperative and necessity of mission.

Independent, Baptist, Methodist and Pentecostal churches never bought into the theology of Christendom in the first place and therefore never embraced a parish system; in these churches membership has always been roll-based and not geography-based. That does not mean to say that such churches are immune from a maintenance mentality: it only means that such churches face fewer structural obstacles if they are minded to move back from maintenance to mission. Everyone is in danger of becoming over-attached to old buildings, but those churches which are more directly descended from Christendom and which still operate a more or less rigid parochial system face additional difficulties in making this transition. In spite of these difficulties, however, change is possible.

The Carpenter's Arms, Deal

Deal is a large town on the Kent coast. It has a diverse population of about 30,000. The local economy is dominated by the
American pharmaceutical firm Pfizer, but there is also the
usual influx of retired people to a coastal town, as well as a
former depot for the Royal Marines. The four parish churches
were doing a reasonable job providing for the needs of the
town's churchgoing Anglicans, according to their various tastes
in churchmanship, but the vicar of St George's, George Lings,
was struggling with two problems. The first was a church that
was already practically full and seemed to have limited scope
for further growth or expansion. The second was a sense that
the Anglican churches of the town, including his own, were
simply not touching some sociological sections of the population. 'Anglican worship,' he used to say, 'is suited to people
from Radio 3 or Radio 4 cultures' – that is, highbrow or at
least middlebrow, musical and literate. How was the Church of
England to communicate with people who listened to Radio 1
or Radio 2, the popular music and easy-listening cultures? The
difference is illustrated within many English homes on a
Sunday evening: the middle-aged parents sitting downstairs in
front of the television watching a programme of community
hymn-singing, *Songs of Praise*; upstairs the teenage children
listening to the week's hit parade of the Top 40 popular songs
on the radio.

Out of these problems came the idea of starting a new
church with a nucleus of people from St George's, to pioneer a
different style of worship and different ways of being church.
The Archdeacon of Canterbury was willing to support the project, even to advocate the investment of diocesan funds in it.
So, in October 1994, a new congregation was launched with
diocesan approval and episcopal blessing, and was named The
Carpenter's Arms.

The new church met in a house called Linwood which had
previously been converted into a youth club by the local

authority. It now had a hall which could seat up to 130, and various other meeting rooms for smaller groups. The Carpenter's Arms hired the premises for the day on Sundays, while the county youth service continued their work in the house throughout the week. For its own weekday activities, The Carpenter's Arms used the homes of members. The Linwood complex was constantly given rough usage by its other regular clients and was often the worse for wear on Sunday mornings, but it was certainly an alternative to the impeccably cared-for Anglican parish churches. Linwood did not lie within the parish of St George's, but in a neighbouring parish, whose priest graciously gave permission for The Carpenter's Arms to meet there. But The Carpenter's Arms was never seen in terms of a cross-boundary church plant, as if it were an outpost of St George's in another parish. It was, rather, a nonboundary church plant, a network church outside the parish system altogether.

The name chosen indicated the sort of atmosphere that the new congregation desired to establish, more that of a pub than a parish church. Instead of sitting in rows of pews, people sat round small tables, café or pub style. Services began with coffee or other soft drinks and crisps for children. No books were handed out or needed by the congregation: all words appeared on the overhead projector. Such a style promoted rather than hindered the making of personal contacts and relationships. It is perfectly possible to sit next to someone in a pew and make no personal contact whatsoever; it is much more difficult to sit round a small table and not talk to each another. The informal atmosphere of the pub or the café was much closer to people's ordinary experience than the solemnity and inhibitions of the parish church.

The new church was led at first by a layman, Alan Dodds. Alan had 25 years' experience as a lay evangelist with the Church Army, British Youth for Christ and Crusaders, and before that had played the guitar as a professional musician in the band of David Bowie. Alan was subsequently ordained; he was obviously equipped to lead a church orientated to mission through the medium of popular culture. At the beginning Alan himself played the guitar, and contemporary Christian songs communicated more directly with the worshippers than organled Victorian hymns.

Alan's wife Chris was a trained teacher and had also led Crusader groups. The couple initiated work among children and young people as a means of outreach to the unchurched: contacts with schools, a club for junior-age children and another for secondary-school children made contacts with whole families. A Christmas pantomime and a parenting course further developed the links and raised the profile of the new congregation in the town. From the beginning The Carpenter's Arms was a child-friendly environment in which children were at home, and because their children were happy, parents tended to be happy too.

The Carpenter's Arms began with a group of 18 adults and 13 children in addition to Alan and Chris Dodds. After 18 months the congregation exceeded 100 for the first time at Easter 1996. By 1999 numbers had reached about 140, a 400 per cent growth in five years. At least a third of this growth was among people who had no previous experience of church. The rest were a mixture of lapsed Christians and some, already Christians, who moved into the area and chose The Carpenter's Arms as their church. Such dynamic growth alone showed that The Carpenter's Arms was fulfilling a spiritual need that the more traditional parish churches were not touching, and justified the original experiment.

By 1999, however, the dynamics of the congregation were beginning to change. The building was becoming too crowded for the café style. The intimacy of a small or middle-sized congregation was being lost in the crowd. The church was facing a new generation of challenges. Alan Dodds felt that it was time to move on and make way for a second generation of leadership. That is a critical transition in the life of a new venture such as this, but The Carpenter's Arms was by then established as a flourishing and growing church.

In 1998 The Carpenter's Arms had acquired the legal status of an 'extraparochial place',[1] making it a self-governing church in its own right, outside the parish system but inside the Church of England. It had become self-financing and by 1998 had achieved the highest per capita giving of any church in the diocese of Canterbury. It was also on the way to being self-propagating. In 1999 The Carpenter's Arms sent out its own group of 20 adults and children to launch a similar project in the town of Sandwich, six miles up the road. This also would be a network church, outside the parish system, deliberately orientated to the task of mission, and drawing on the lessons and values learned through The Carpenter's Arms.

Thus, in five or six years, one, even two, new churches had been planted alongside the old ones on the coast of Kent. The Carpenter's Arms had the freedom to experiment with a different style of meeting and worship, and with different ways of being church. The parish churches and the other churches in the town went on as before. The Carpenter's Arms did not involve taking away from anybody things which they already valued or to which they had already become attached, whether it was organs, hymns, liturgies, pews or Gothic arches. The old was still honoured for what it was, but it no longer impeded new growth and new missionary endeavours. The Carpenter's Arms showed that the obstacles to structural renewal in the Church of England could be overcome.

*   *   *

---

1 The 'extraparochial place' is a device in Anglican church law which removes a designated place from the control of the parish church. See Pastoral Measure 1983 17 (i) (d).

Imi Kirken, Stavanger, Norway

The city of Stavanger is the heart of a conurbation on the south-west coast of Norway, with a total population of around 200,000. It is a centre of the Norwegian North Sea oil industry. At the end of the eighteenth century Norway experienced a revival, similar in many ways to the Wesleyan revival in Britain. Norway's Wesley was a man called Hans Nielsen Hauge (1771–1824). Being a layman, Hauge was imprisoned more than once for usurping the privilege of the clergy by preaching. His typical preaching was to small groups of men, women and children in homes and farmsteads, the weather in Norway being even more unkind to open-air preaching than it is in England. In spite of the persecution that Hauge suffered, he remained faithful to the state church, and he urged his converts and followers to do the same.

Hauge's ministry developed into a missionary movement which had a remarkable impact both on Norway and on Norway's outreach to the world. Out of this impetus came the Norwegian Missionary Society, founded in 1842, under whose auspices an extraordinary number of people from such a small population have gone, and continue to go, overseas to serve the Lord. In Norway itself Hauge's house meetings grew into prayer houses: what we in Britain would call chapels. These chapels formed themselves into connections and organisations which devoted themselves to the evangelisation of Norway, to home mission. One such organisation was the Indremisjon.

During the nineteenth and twentieth centuries these prayer houses continued to multiply across the land, but, faithful to the inspiration of Hauge, they maintained their connection with the established church. Their members remain members of the state church, typically attending the parish church in the morning and the prayer house in the evening, and resorting to their parish churches to receive the sacraments of baptism, confirmation and Holy Communion. Prayer house services are, as their name suggests, meetings for prayer, Bible reading and preaching. Though sometimes attended by the parish clergy themselves, the prayer houses have never developed an ordained ministry of their own and have never come directly under the authority of the bishop; in a curious way they are, as they say, 'in the church but not under the church'. In any given parish there may be one or several such prayer houses, several especially in parishes where the parish church is remote or inaccessible.

One such prayer house was established under the Indremisjon in Stavanger in 1876. By 1979 this fellowship had declined to a small congregation of faithful people, who nevertheless had the vision to invite Martin Cave to join them as their organising secretary. Martin was a young schoolteacher in the city with a passion for evangelism among young people. A layman like Hauge, Martin Cave has now led this one-time prayer house for 23 years, through many stages of development and renewal, retaining the same zeal for the evangelisation of the young of Stavanger, until today it is one of the largest Lutheran churches in Norway.

By 1987 the work had outgrown the original white-painted, wooden prayer house and the congregation moved down the street to a new office block. The upper storeys were let to the government, while the fellowship retained the ground floor and basement as a worship centre, meeting rooms and offices for their own use. By 1996 even this building was proving to be inadequate, as the congregation continued to grow and the work to expand. At this point, in partnership with the civic authorities and a commercial hotel company, the church embarked on a project of breathtaking boldness and imagination – to develop land in another part of the city to provide not just a worship arena and facilities for the church, but also an international conference centre and a 182-room, 22-storey luxury hotel. In 2001 the Stavanger Indremisjon, now known as Imi Kirken, opened this new complex, with an arena seating 1,850 people and café and restaurants to match, as well as a chapel and rooms for the smaller meetings and activities of the congregation, its Bible School and offices. The church's adult membership now stands at 500, with a multitude of children and young people in addition. At the opening service of the new buildings there was a congregation of over 1,000.

With an ultramodern worship style and an overtly charismatic spirituality, Imi Kirken is very different from the traditional Lutheran parish churches around it. This church has grown largely by the conversion of the unchurched and the non-Christian, people with no previous allegiance to a parish church and for whom Imi Kirken is the only church they have ever known. Faithful to the old prayer house tradition, Imi Kirken still does not hold any morning services in competition with the parish churches, but for the majority of its members the Imi evening services are the only ones they ever attend. By a strange twist of providence, the Imi Kirken now finds itself in step with the way of life of young twenty-first-century Norwegians: after a Saturday night out, this generation appreciates its Sunday morning lie-in, its leisurely breakfast, a family trip into the mountains to ski, or a visit to friends or relations, before the church service at 6.00 p.m.

Recognising that Imi Kirken is a church in its own right in all but name, the bishop has for ten years permitted the celebration of Holy Communion in the church (not under the presidency of Martin Cave, but led by an ordained minister who belongs to the congregation). In the last two years he has also permitted baptisms to take place there (provided they are counted as taking place at the parish church), and in the last year he has permitted Imi Kirken to prepare and hold its own confirmation for young people. It is now the bishop's desire to ordain Martin as a priest in the Lutheran Church, and at that point the Imi Kirken's transition from a prayer house to a Lutheran church will be complete. Imi Kirken will still be an anomaly in the state church, a church without a parish in the midst of a parish system at least as rigid and legalistic as the English one.

The Norwegian church in the nineteenth century devised in the prayer house movement a mechanism whereby the dynamism of revival and the passion for mission could be expressed within the life of the established church; the parallel structures of prayer houses and parish churches held together the church's functions of maintenance and mission. Such is the nature of humanity and its institutions that by the second half of the twentieth century the prayer houses as much as the parish churches had developed their own preoccupation with maintenance, and they, as much as the parish churches, have resisted the latest move of God's Spirit in the charismatic renewal. However, in the Imi Kirken in Stavanger God is once again breaking through the tendency to ossification in both prayer house and parish structures and creating a new hybrid: an extraparochial Lutheran church. The Spirit of God is ever zealous to bring Christ to the lost and the loveless, and ever zealous, in the words of the old Moravians, 'to win for the Lamb the reward of his sufferings'. For this purpose he is always breaking down old structures and building new ones.

* * *

New communities, France

For 1,500 years since the collapse of the Roman Empire, the spiritual centre of gravity of the Catholic Church has lain in the religious communities, the monasteries and nunneries. It was monks who re-evangelised Europe during the Dark Ages. It was the celibate monk or nun who remained the dominant role model of the Christian life throughout the Middle Ages. And all the movements of spiritual renewal that found acceptance in the church during the Middle Ages took the form of a renewal of the conventual life. Even the movement associated with Francis of Assisi, so unecclesiastical in its original inspiration, ended up as a new order of monks, or friars. It is not surprising, therefore, that the modern charismatic renewal in the

Catholic Church has found expression in the creation of new religious communities.

Many of these new communities and movements have originated in France, and have spread rapidly throughout the world: L'Emmanuel, Les Béatitudes and Le Chemin Neuf (The New Way) were all founded in the 1970s; others like Le Verbe de Vie (The Word of Life) followed in the 1980s. The Community of the Beatitudes now has 80 houses worldwide. These new communities sprang up from the grass roots; they established themselves within the existing parochial, diocesan or community structures of the church. Some of them are now sufficiently well formed to be seeking independent recognition from the Pope. They seek to serve the church in co-operation with local bishops, parish priests and other religious houses, even though they may be outside their authority.

What distinguishes these new communities from the older, more traditional Catholic communities is, first, that they are overtly charismatic. In the Community of the Beatitudes, for example, the evening office of Vespers may begin with five minutes of corporate singing in tongues, and end with personal prayer and the laying on of hands for those who are sick. But the new communities are different in a more radical way: unlike the older communities, strictly single-sex, living a life of poverty, chastity and obedience, more or less secluded from the world outside, these new communities are a conscious and deliberate mixture of men and women, of priests and lay people, of the celibate and the married. The house of the Community of the Beatitudes in Cuisery in Burgundy includes monks and nuns, a priest as well as lay brothers and sisters, and it is pastored by a married couple with children, the whole community living a common life, eating, worshipping and working together. Chemin Neuf is even more radical, including within it on equal terms not only Catholic but Protestant and Orthodox Christians, ordained and lay, married and single, monks, nuns and families.

Not all these new movements are religious communities in

the strict sense of the word. Le Verbe de Vie, for example, has five houses in France, Belgium and Switzerland, but also about 40 fraternities, or small groups, which meet together on a fortnightly basis in each other's houses, to pray together, to share a meal and to study the Bible. These fraternities include both priests and lay people, in ordinary parishes, ordinary homes and ordinary jobs. Being part of Le Verbe de Vie offers its adherents opportunities for spiritual development and training, through retreats and conferences, through family and youth festivals in the summer, and an accountability and fellowship not normally found in the local parish church.

The Catholic Church in France, like the Church of England, is the heir to both the theory and the organisation of Christendom. Its dioceses and parishes cover the whole nation, it has a legacy of church buildings in almost every town and village (although in France many of these buildings are maintained by the state), and the continuing expectation of infant baptisms, marriages and funerals for many people who have otherwise given up the Christian faith and its practices. The diocesan and parochial structures of the Catholic Church in France face exactly the same problems as the Church of England, except on an even graver scale. The shortage of priests is even more desperate, the supply of young diocesan priests having almost completely dried up and many older priests now entering retirement. Radical pastoral reorganisation has been forced on the dioceses: the diocese of Grenoble, for example, recently regrouped its 546 old parishes into 45 new ones overnight.

In the early days of charismatic renewal in France, many charismatic prayer groups were formed in the parishes. Few of these have flourished in the longer term. For want of leadership and encouragement many of them are now elderly and declining, and they have never achieved any real breakthrough in the life of the parish churches. As in England, diocesan bishops and parish priests are often fearful and suspicious of charismatics and prefer to ignore, if not actively suppress, this new movement of God's Spirit. It is not surprising that the river of renewal in the Catholic Church in France has run instead into the new communities and fraternities.

These new communities have often taken over old monastic buildings. Thus Chemin Neuf took over the Benedictine monastery at Hautecombe in the French Alps, after the monks had moved further south into Provence for the sake of a quiet life. Many other such buildings, however, formerly inhabited by older traditional communities, have simply become redundant, as vocations have dwindled and communities have died out. The more spectacular of these are preserved as museums or as part of the national heritage by the French government.

In the Catholic Church religious communities have always been a sort of parallel church alongside the diocesan and parochial structures. In Christendom, while the parish churches ministered to everybody in society, the religious communities retained the character of a church called out of the surrounding society, membership of which entailed a conscious and deliberate choice and commitment. In this sense the new charismatic communities are truly the heirs of this older Catholic tradition, providing alternative structures to the regular parochial ones, structures which can contain and nurture a hunger for God which the parish churches are simply not satisfying.

There are all the same signs in France as in England that the parish system is on the point of collapse. Alongside the older structures in France, however, new communities have recently emerged which show signs of growth and vitality. It is the new charismatic communities such as those mentioned above that are producing most of the vocations, both to the priesthood and to the religious life, and seeing most of the conversions from secularism to Christianity. The new communities, unlike the older religious communities, are open to and able to minister to lay people, married couples and families; they are the beginnings of a new church growing up alongside the old one.

*   *   *

Fountain of Life

The history of the Fountain of Life has been told earlier in this book. It is now an independent congregation, separate from the parish churches out of which it came, with a new worship centre of its own in the process of being built. The scheme by which this has been accomplished proposes the establishment of a formal team ministry encompassing the local market town, four surrounding villages, including our own two former parishes, and the Fountain of Life as a sixth, nonparochial congregation. The ministerial team will consist formally of a team rector who is the rector of the market town, and two team vicars, one my successor in the village churches, the other myself, a team vicar with particular responsibility for the Fountain of Life alone. The premises of the Fountain of Life in the former garage will become an 'extraparochial place'.

This arrangement represents a closer relationship between the Fountain of Life and the surrounding parish churches than is the case with The Carpenter's Arms in Deal. It ensures that the Fountain of Life continues to take notice of the fact that there are surrounding Anglican parish churches, and conversely that the parish churches take notice of the existence of an extraparochial Anglican congregation, the Fountain of Life. This is intended to encourage a healthy working relationship and a measure of co-operation between the parties concerned.

For the regulation of relationships between the Fountain of Life and the parish churches, the following set of protocols was drawn up and agreed.

Protocols for the Relationship of the Fountain of Life to Neighbouring Parish Churches

Fountain of Life

1. Fountain of Life is a missionary congregation of the Church of England, holding a charismatic doctrine of the baptism of the Holy Spirit, seeking to develop distinctive, alternative

forms of worship and church life, with a view to making the church attractive and accessible to some people who would otherwise be unchurched or unbelievers, especially in the younger generation.

2. Fountain of Life is an extraparochial church, serving its own members, and reaching out to the unchurched and unbelievers through the networks of relationships which its members have with their neighbours at home, at work, and at leisure, with families and friends.

3. The main thrust of the Fountain of Life is evangelism through personal contact, through worship, through the fellowship of the church community, through preaching and teaching (particularly through the Alpha course), through the ministry of signs and wonders, and through works of mercy and service.

Attitude to parish churches in the area

1. Fountain of Life will not seek to poach worshippers from other churches. However, Fountain of Life cannot turn people away who wish to come.

2. Fountain of Life will seek ways of co-operating with other churches, in common witness, in serving the community at large, and from time to time in shared worship.

3. Fountain of Life will seek to be a catalyst in encouraging and enabling other churches to be mission orientated in their own way. We would expect in time to see other churches in the area growing as a result of the stimulus of the presence of the Fountain of Life.

4. Fountain of Life would hope to be able to resource other churches, offering any gifts or skills that they might have or develop.

5. In all these things, Fountain of Life does not wish to live and work in isolation from other churches, but to be a blessing to other Christians and churches round about.

Technical matters

1. The home for the Fountain of Life will be at The Well Christian Centre, Swaffham Road, Ashill. Ashill is the centre of gravity of the congregation and that is where God started this work. The Well is where God has made room for us.

2. Fountain of Life will maintain its own membership roll, composed of those who:
   - are 16 years of age or over
   - have been baptised in water in the name of the Trinity
   - have attended worship at Fountain of Life for at least six months
   - apply for enrolment

3. The children of such members will be baptised at the request of their parents at Fountain of Life; adults who wish to become members but who have not already been baptised, will be baptised at Fountain of Life; but all such baptisms will be entered in the parish register of the parish in which they take place. All other requests for baptism will be referred to the parish priest of the appropriate parish.

4. Arrangements may be made for members to be married at Fountain of Life, but all requests for marriage from non-members will be referred to the appropriate parish priest.

5. Funeral services may be conducted for members, but all requests for funerals from non-members will be referred to the appropriate parish priest. Fountain of Life will have no burial ground of its own.

6. Fountain of Life will seek appropriate representation on the Deanery Synod, and its clergy and lay people will seek to play a full part in the Deanery Synod and Chapter.

7. Fountain of Life will be fully self-supporting financially, and will pay whatever diocesan share is agreed with the diocesan authorities.

8. Fountain of Life will keep accounts which will be submitted annually to an independent auditor or examiner, and if

necessary to the Charity Commissioners.

9. Ordained ministers of Fountain of Life will observe the usual courtesies towards clergy in the parishes, only visiting those who attend Fountain of Life or others by whom they are specifically invited.

At the time of writing it is not clear how well such an arrangement will work in the long run. The essence of the situation is that we are all finding our way in a new landscape. The Fountain of Life is a cuckoo in the nest, and it is not clear how well the little birds will thrive together. It all depends on relationships.

People with some historical awareness of the origins of the Methodist chapels in our villages realise that we have been here before, that the Church of England was faced with similar dilemmas in the eighteenth and nineteenth centuries as the effects of the Wesleyan revival spread across the land. Then, the tide of spiritual renewal overflowed the parish churches or found the parish churches sandbagged against it, so it flowed into the chapels. It was Wesley's hope to his dying day that somehow the Methodist movement could be contained within the Church of England, of which he lived and died a minister. Then, it was not to be. But there is hope that this time around the church has learned the lessons of that previous revival and will be more imaginative and determined in overcoming the obstacles to the renewal of the structures.

*   *   *

We have looked at four examples drawn from different parts of Europe, where the legacy of Christendom is a parish system and the particular relationship with the community which goes with it. We have seen how in each case the dynamic of renewal in the church has led both historically and contemporarily to the creation of new structures alongside the old ones, structures designed to facilitate the renewed mission of the church. The imperative of mission and the demands of maintenance have both been so great that out of the tension between them have emerged new ideas and realities that have within them the shape of a new church alongside the old one.

11

Distinct Communities

In the present age the church is called by Jesus not to be coterminous or co-extensive with the world, but to be a distinct and distinctive community within the world. This is a very different understanding from that of Christendom in which, in Hooker's words, church and commonwealth are one and the same body of people under two different aspects. This may be an alluring theory, but it involves either reverting to an Old Testament model of church and society that belongs to the age before Christ, or anticipating a model of church and society that belongs to the age to come when Christ returns. Neither model is applicable to this present age, between the first and second comings of Christ.

Jesus used two pictures or parables of the present relationship of the church and the world: those of salt and light.

> You are the salt of the earth. But if the salt loses its saltiness, how can it be made salty again? It is no longer good for anything, except to be thrown out and trampled by men.
>
> You are the light of the world. A city on a hill cannot be hidden. Neither do people light a lamp and put it under a bowl. Instead they put it on its stand, and it gives light to everyone in the house. In the same way, let your light shine before men, that they may see your good deeds and praise your Father in heaven. (Matthew 5:13–16)

The distinctions between the salt and the earth, and between the light and the world, are crucial, and are emphasised by Jesus. If the salt loses its distinctiveness, its saltiness, it is no longer good for anything; it reverts to being part of the earth which it was supposed to season. If the light ceases to shine in the surrounding darkness of the world, it might as well not exist; the light of the disciples of Jesus must shine before the rest of the human race. The distinctiveness of the church from the rest of the world around it must be maintained and must be made manifest.

For the Church of England, and for other established churches, this requires a radical change in the way in which we perceive ourselves and our relationship to society. Such a change in perception has already begun in society itself, but it is less advanced in the church. As it advances in both, it must lead to changes in the law and the legal relationship between church and state. Once again we find ourselves, both in church and state, living at the present time with split minds on this subject. At one and the same time the Church of England is perceived as just another religious institution – its active membership a small minority in the country, perhaps an even smaller minority than the Muslims; its active membership even a minority in the Christian community in the country, perhaps an even smaller minority than the Roman Catholics – and yet the Church of England is still the institution to which society continues to turn to express its corporate emotions of sorrow and joy. After the death of a princess, or a rail crash, or even a simple family bereavement, it is to the established church that most people still turn to provide the solemnities the occasion seems to require. Yet in the politically correct realm of the school curriculum, Christianity is no more than one among five of the world's major religions, and the Church of England no more than one among many different expressions of Christianity.

There does not seem, however, to be any doubt in which direction society is moving. The assumption that the Church of

England and even Christianity has a special place in society
belongs to the past, to the older generation, and to the Church
of England itself; the relativist, pluralist understanding of society belongs to the future, to the young, and to those of other
denominations and religions. Of this development Christianity
and, indeed, the Church of England should not be afraid. We
have been here before, in the first three centuries of Christian
history, and these were the days of the church's greatest vigour
and expansion. This is surely where the church of Jesus Christ
is supposed to be: a part of society but not the whole. There is
among the older generation of Christians in England a linger-
ing resentment or sense of scandal about what is perceived as
the marginalisation of the church and of Christianity in society. There is still a feeling that the nation's schools should be
doing the church's job, and indoctrinating the children into
Christianity, if not still teaching them to memorise the Prayer
Book collects. There is also a more justifiable fear of what
might take the place of Christianity in the life of the nation, if
the Church of England were finally squeezed out of its historic
position. But rather than clinging on to unjustifiable privileges
of doubtful spiritual value, let us more positively embrace the
philosophy of that secular society which has emerged
from Christendom, and which does no more and no less than
God did at the beginning: grants to all of us the right to choose
our gods.

Instead of resenting the freedom that secular society gives to
its citizens to embrace Islam or Judaism, Hinduism or
Buddhism, atheism, druidism, or simply shopping, as their way
of life, let us rejoice in the freedom that it gives us to embrace
Christianity and to worship and witness to the God and Father
of our Lord Jesus Christ. This is not a freedom that can be
taken for granted, as a glance round the world will quickly
confirm. There are many worse scenarios in which to be a
Christian than a secular society. This is another example of
how we Christians need to let go of our nostalgia for the past
and an unscriptural ideology and discover that there is a better

way, and indeed an older way, to be the church in the world.

Sooner or later such a change of outlook must involve changes to the terms of the establishment of the Church of England, if not, as in Ireland and Wales, to outright disestablishment. Everyone today is ambivalent about the place of the sovereign as titular head of the church. Christians are much more sensitive today than perhaps they were in the past about the moral and spiritual integrity of those who have been, or who are, or who might be supreme governors of the church. It is a strange constitutional arrangement which grants freedom of religion to everyone in the land except certain members of one family. To many people outside it there is now no obvious reason why the Church of England should occupy such a privileged position in the realm as opposed to any other church or even any other religion. We are in the midst of a sort of creeping constitutional crisis, which in a typically English way will probably be resolved by evolution rather than revolution. The reform of the House of Lords and the issues raised by Prince Charles will be steps along the way in that process. It will not be easy, however, to resolve the contradictions in our present arrangements.

At the local, but probably even more contentious, level the Church of England needs to establish clearer boundaries for itself. We have seen before that it is no service to people to obscure the fact that entry into the kingdom of God requires of an adult a personal decision to repent and believe in the gospel. No one enters the kingdom of heaven by default. We have also seen how mischievous can be the involvement of people outside the church in its government. The Church of England only scandalises the Christians inside it and confuses the non-Christians outside it when it solemnly baptises the babies of people whose lifestyle is flagrantly at odds with God's commandments, and solemnly presides over the burial of notorious criminals who have shown no repentance or remorse. The Book of Common Prayer never intended or envisaged such abuses.

No church can maintain its integrity or its witness without a workable system of discipline, and no system of discipline is workable without some identifiable boundary separating those without from those within the church. The Church of England, like every other church, is supposed to have such a system, and it is enshrined in the Book of Common Prayer, but it has fallen into disuse. Membership of the church today should be defined by enrolment not by residence. Enrolment should depend on more than someone's age and involuntary infant baptism. The least that should be required is an adult profession of faith, say confirmation, and the maintenance year by year of communicant status. When one recalls the teaching of Jesus about what it means to be a disciple, such conditions for membership of the church are the bare minimum of outward conformity. But only church members defined in some such way should have any entitlement to the rites and sacraments of the church such as baptisms, marriages or funerals.

Such a discipline would not prevent a local church from entertaining requests from nonmembers for such services. Such requests could still be used as pastoral opportunities and occasions for evangelism. But ministers would have a pastoral discretion about such requests and a right to respect of which at present they are deprived. Nothing rots the consciences of the clergy of the Church of England so much as their legal obligation continually to perform Christian ceremonies for people who are manifestly ungodly and irreligious.

To members of the Church of England such notions will seem at variance with the ethos of the church, but in every other church and everywhere else even in the Anglican Communion, they would seem to be both scriptural and common sense. In the Episcopal Church of the United States of America, the Anglican Church in the USA, membership is roll-based; there are no geographical parishes; only those with current communicant status are allowed to take part in the government of the church; applications for baptisms, marriages, funerals or other forms of pastoral care are sympathetically received, but everyone knows that an extension of such pastoral care is a grace not a right. Even within the Anglican world one has to ask the question, 'Which soldier is out of step?'

When our Fountain of Life congregation came out of the parish church in 1996, we inadvertently stepped out of the whole parish system. The result is that in this extraparochial Anglican fellowship we are no longer obliged to perform Christian ceremonies, indeed we are expressly forbidden to perform them, for the population at large. We are only allowed to minister in such ways to our own enrolled members. Thus, as I said before, with one bound Jack was free, not only of the responsibility for and the conflict of interest involved in historic buildings, but also of the legal and ceremonial entanglements of Christendom. We are now in the position, not of an Anglican parish church, but of any other church in England or any other branch of the Anglican Church throughout the world. Everyone is clear about who our members are and who they are not. We are a community with recognisable boundaries, distinct from the society round about us.

*   *   *

Many people are anxious about such disengagement from society. They fear that the church will become sectarian, closed and inward-looking, 'a holy huddle'. Never mind that this is exactly what many of our parish churches already are. Never mind that this was and is the danger faced by all the nonestablished churches in the world. It is a real danger. One has only to look at some congregations of Strict and Particular Baptists or some congregations of the Brethren to see that such a narrowing of vision is possible. But it is not inevitable. To recognise ourselves to be not the whole, but simply a part of society does not necessarily entail that we end up apart from society.

The church is called to be a distinct community and that distinctness requires boundaries and disciplines. A distinct community is not, however, necessarily a closed community or a disengaged community. The church is called to be distinct, but also to be open to and involved with the world around it. Such openness and involvement should be expressed in two main ways, which should be part of the discipleship both of individual Christians and of the church corporately: works of witness and works of mercy and service.

The primary calling of the church in a missionary situation is to witness to the saving work of Jesus Christ, in season, as Paul says to Timothy, and out of season (2 Timothy 4:2). Many and any means should be used. There is still a place for the set-piece mission or crusade. For nearly 50 years such expressions of mission and evangelism were almost synonymous with Billy Graham, but others have succeeded him. J. John is running very successful missions based on the Ten Commandments. Other itinerant preachers, often from a Pentecostal background, combine gospel preaching with a public ministry of healing.

Alpha is a particularly modern, or postmodern, means of evangelism, relying on an inspired mix of evangelistic preaching and teaching, hospitality and friendship, and the opportunity to talk and think our beliefs through in a nonthreatening environment. God knows, there may still be a place for open-air preaching such as Whitefield and Wesley used to bring the gospel to eighteenth-century Britain. Whatever public or organised forms of evangelism we may use or devise, the key to their effectiveness, and ultimately the most effective of them all, is personal evangelism: the recommendation of Jesus to one individual by another within an existing and ongoing relationship of trust and respect.

The most extended study of personal evangelism in the Bible is found in John 4:1–42, where Jesus engages a woman of Samaria in conversation at the well. Christians have to find the way to the wells of today, the places where non-Christians are encountered. It is a sign of the church becoming disengaged from the world when Christians spend all their time with other Christians. We must find our way to the wells where people meet and talk. What will bring us together is a common need, like thirst, or a common interest. It is important that the need or interest is a genuine one on our part, as was Jesus' thirst, and not a mere camouflage for a different agenda.

With such a genuine need and interest in common, conversation with non-Christians is not difficult, but there is still a barrier to be crossed between talking about the mundane and talking about spiritual things, between talking about drinking water and talking about Jesus. Christians are not fully engaging with the world while they keep their conversations separate, talking about worldly things with worldly people and about Christ only with Christian people. The challenge which Jesus sets us by his example is to talk about him to worldly people in such a way as to catch their attention and interest.

The breakthrough with the Samaritan woman comes when Jesus reveals to her a supernatural knowledge of her past and present affairs with men: 'You have had five husbands, and the man you now have is not your husband' (v. 18). The setting for Jesus' use of the supernatural gifts of the Holy Spirit is nearly always like this, in public places and unexpected encounters. Our present expectation that God will impart gifts of the Holy Spirit at the end of worship services and Christian meetings does not correspond with the life and ministry of Jesus. John Wimber used to say that 'the meeting place is the learning place for the market place'. Too often we Christians never seem to venture out of the meeting place or the learning place and trust God for gifts of the Spirit in the market place.

The work of witness is not complete, however, until we have presented someone with the challenge of believing in Jesus and responding to his call. Again we are not fully engaging with the world if we fail to make the ultimate claim of Jesus clear, and do not give people the opportunity to receive him as their Lord and Saviour.

There are other forms of engagement with the world to which we are called, though these are not a substitute for the work of witness. Jesus fed the multitude, probably on more than one occasion. This was not an alternative to teaching or preaching to them; on the contrary, it was in the context of teaching and preaching to them. He simply had compassion on them (Mark 6:34; 8:2). It was the same compassion which led Jesus to teach the crowds and to feed them. In the same way, any love and compassion we feel for our neighbours will lead us both to works of witness and to works of mercy and service, both to tell people about the Saviour and to minister to their needs.

The traditional works of mercy are enumerated in the parable of the sheep and the goats (Matthew 26:31–46): they are to feed the hungry and give drink to the thirsty, to shelter the stranger, to clothe the ragged, to care for the sick and visit those in prison. Even in a modern welfare state there are plenty of opportunities for Christians to show compassion in these ways. Giving money to charitable societies for their work at home or abroad is an important aspect of showing compassion, but so also is personal involvement with the needy in our own localities.

An awareness and sensitivity towards the needs of our own neighbours will certainly produce opportunities to help and serve them: the needs of the elderly, in times of illness or in bad weather, the needs of single parents working and bringing up children on their own, the needs of young couples for babysitters. Imagination and generosity of heart will enable us to show God's love and compassion to our neighbours regardless of their disposition towards him.

Such is the increased pace of life and the pressure of work today that organisations which depend on volunteers are always short of helpers. There are many opportunities for Christians to be involved in such works if they are willing to sacrifice the time: taking old people meals-on-wheels; assisting with children's groups and activities in school or out of school;

visiting in prisons; and, in rural areas especially, driving the car-less on essential journeys.

There may be gaps in the provision of official and voluntary social services which a local church may be able to fill. Many city churches provide a soup kitchen for the homeless; some churches run a second-hand furniture store; others again make their premises available for playschools or luncheon clubs. It can be productive and illuminating for a local church to conduct an audit, first of the local community and its needs, and second of the gifts and availability of its members to meet those needs.

A modern secular society gives its citizens many opportunities to be engaged in the working of its institutions, opportunities from which Christians are not debarred any more than anyone else. The political process requires extensive participation by the people, not only as voters, but as members of political parties and as candidates for election. Schools offer opportunities for service as governors or members of home-school associations. Trades unions, chambers of commerce, professional associations, the Women's Institute and the golf club all depend on public-spirited people serving as committee members and office holders.

The opportunities for Christians to be engaged with the society and the communities in which they live are infinite. We may have to renounce the idea of a Christian society, but we certainly do not have to renounce the idea of being a Christian influence in and on our society. Indeed, that is our calling: to be salt and light.

* * *

The following are examples, all drawn from our own congregation, the Fountain of Life, of individuals fulfilling this calling in ways in which each one feels equipped and called by God.

(None of these examples involves a person's paid employment. To consider paid employment as an expression of our engagement in society and as an opportunity to serve others would open up vistas for us as Christians which are hugely important but beyond the scope of this book.) This is not meant to be an exhaustive list, merely an indication of the ways in which the members of one church are functioning as salt and light in their communities.

Peter is chairman of the local Conservative Association.

Christine stood as a candidate for the Green Party in county council elections.

Brian is a parish councillor.

Peter is a co-ordinator of his local Home Watch scheme.

Dan, Val, Martin and Brenda are governors of local schools.

Colette is chair of her village playgroup committee.

Martin is chairman of his village youth club.

Bryony is Brown Owl of the Brownie pack.

Jean and John serve on the management committees of their respective village community centres.

Jim is an adviser for the Citizens' Advice Bureau.

Pippa visits an old lady under the auspices of Age Concern to help her with money matters.

Pat is chair of the Patients' Participation Group at the doctor's surgery.

Mike is a trustee of the Refuge for Battered Women.

Jean is a carer for the home hospice.

Rosie is on the committee of her town's swimming pool association.

Ron and Rachel visit in the local prison.

Grace helps to run the old people's luncheon club.

Vera drives for the community car scheme.

Jenny works in a charity shop in the high street.

12

Distinctive Communities

It is necessary for the church to be a distinct community in society, distinct in the sense of separate. But it is also necessary for the church to be a distinctive community, distinctive in the sense of different. The church must have something distinctive to offer society, or else why should society be interested in the church at all? In the King James Version of the Bible, Peter says that Christians are 'a peculiar people' (1 Peter 2:9). Modern translations, such as 'a people belonging to God' (NIV), may do more justice to the original Greek, but the fact remains that a people belonging to God should in some sense be peculiar or different.

There is, however, more than one way of being peculiar, and it is important for Christians and for the church to sort out the ways in which they are supposed to be different from the ways in which they are supposed to be the same. The dilemma was first posed by Jesus. In his prayer on the night that he was betrayed, Jesus declared that his disciples were not 'of the world', though they would still be 'in the world'; his prayer was not that the Father would 'take them out of the world', for indeed he was sending them 'into the world' (John 17:11–18). It is only too easy for us to be glib about being in the world but not of the world. We have not thought carefully enough about how to do it. To put the dilemma in modern terms, in what

139

ways should the church be in tune with the culture (in the world), and in what ways should it be countercultural (not of the world)?

It could be said that too often the church is the same as the world in ways in which it should be different, and different from the world in ways that it should be the same. The church dresses its ministers and choirs up in robes that have not been seen in the world since the decline and fall of the Roman Empire, but too often church members are as caught up in the culture of greed and lust as any of their worldly neighbours. To be in the world and yet not of the world is a more challenging exercise of our faith than we often suppose. Once again, we are afraid that being different from the world will cut us off from the world and cause us to lose touch with it – and it can do. So we congratulate ourselves on being 'normal' and 'human', when what we mean is that we are only too worldly and sinful. By whose standards are we 'normal' or 'human', by the standards of the world or by the standard of Jesus, the Son of Man?

The life of the church is more than the lives of individual Christians, however. Not only do we need to order our individual lives by a different set of values from the world, but the life of the church should also reflect values which are countercultural. Some people advocate new forms of church on the basis that they are in conformity with contemporary culture. In as much as these people are motivated by the desire to reach and penetrate the culture with the gospel, we need to listen to them. But in the end the form of the church needs to be determined not by cultural but by scriptural values. We can become so formed by our own culture that we lose the distinctiveness that is required of us by the gospel. It must be Scripture that indicates to us how and where the church is to be incarnate in, or assimilated to, the prevailing culture, and how and where the church is to be different and distinctive.

Here are seven scriptural ways in which I believe the church should be countercultural today. The church should be:

- *A place of love.* Without love we are nothing (1 Corinthians 13:1–3). Our culture is increasingly impersonal; its focus is on possessions and technology rather than on people. You can love a new pair of shoes, for a few days, but a new pair of shoes can never love you. Even personal communication is increasingly impersonal as people correspond on the internet and the mobile phone. The computer can give you access to everything you want to know, and more, but the computer does not know you. The church should be a place where people are known, and loved, and given a hug.

- *A new community.* The Scriptures show us the church as a place where the dividing walls between people are broken down, between young and old (Psalm 148:12; Malachi 4:5–6), between Jew and Gentile, slave and free, male and female (Galatians 3:28). Our culture is increasingly fragmented. As we have seen, local geographical communities have been dissolved by the motor car. The primary community of the family is increasingly breaking down. More and more people of all ages are living on their own. Friends are very often more important today than family, but many people have no friends. Many of the networks to which people belong are narrowly age- or interest-based. The church needs to build new communities; not to try to rebuild the old communities which have broken down, but to be a new community in itself. The church should be an integrative community, bringing together those whom the world and the culture separate, the young and the old, the rich and the poor, the black and the white, breaking down, not reinforcing, the dividing walls that keep individuals and groups isolated.

- *A bulwark of the truth* (1 Timothy 3:15). Postmodern culture has abandoned the concept of truth. Truth is reduced to a matter of taste or choice. People go shopping for beliefs or for morals in much the same way as they go shopping for dinners or trousers. A religion or a way of life is made up as you go along: a bit of this and a bit of that. Whether it suits me or fits me is the only criterion of acceptability. But the church believes in truth. There is one living and true God, and Jesus Christ whom he sent is the Truth – about God, about ourselves, and about our relationship to God and to one another.

- *An economy of grace.* There are three economies in the world, all operating side by side, but few people, even economists, can see the difference. First there is the world's economy of buying and selling, in which everything has its price. There is nothing wrong with this economy and the world could not function without it. The second economy is the devil's economy, which is characterised by getting something for nothing. It is an immensely popular economy even with those who do not benefit from it. It is the economy not only of theft and fraud, but of gambling and the National Lottery, and of much of the dealing in stocks and shares, foreign currencies and commodities. The third economy is God's economy, and it consists of giving something for nothing. It is the economy of grace. The church needs to explore what it means to live in this economy, not only as recipients of the grace of God, but as dispensers of grace to one another (1 Peter 4:10). In the apostolic church, 'selling their possessions and goods, they gave to anyone as he had need' (Acts 2:45). We have little idea what that looks like today, but we need to find out.

- *A place of balance and rhythm.* If there is one factor common to most people's lives today, it is stress. The world has let go of, or overridden, the balances and rhythm built into life by nature. The day for toil, the night for rest; but electric light makes possible, and industrial processes make necessary, a regime where day and night cease to count. As the power of trades unions has been eroded, so has people's protection against pressure and exploitation at work: increasingly every day of the year is an ordinary working day. We are becoming a 24/7 society. The church should be faithful to the principle of the Sabbath as a shared day of rest, rest shared with God and with one another (Exodus 20:8–11). The pattern and rhythm given to our lives by one day of rest in seven, and by the seasonal festivals of the Christian year, are important antidotes to the monotony and drudgery of life.

- *A support for marriage.* In an incredibly short time, about ten years, the institution of Christian marriage as the bedrock of society fell apart in Britain. Divorce had been increasing for decades, but all of a sudden, in the 1990s, 'partners' took the place of husbands and wives, and cohabitation took the place of marriage. At the same time pressure has enormously increased for society to recognise homosexual relationships as equivalent to heterosexual ones. As social disciplines supporting marriage have broken down, so much more should the church's discipline continue to uphold it. The church should be distinctive as a place where the idea of a lifelong union of one man and one woman to the exclusion of all others is still believed in and encouraged (Genesis 2:24), and where people can still see attractive models of it being lived out in practice.

- *A people of the Book.* The Reformation churches at least have always been people of the Book. In our culture the book is often discounted as a medium of communication, in favour of more visual and electronic means. Images are valued more than words and screens more than pages, and indeed we need to learn to use all these media to convey the message of the gospel. But the church should remain resolutely attached to its book, the Bible. It should continue to read it aloud publicly and encourage people to read it privately, to mark it, learn it, and inwardly digest it. Nothing in modern culture can be a substitute for God's book (2 Timothy 3:16–17).

None of this is irrelevant to the missionary task of the church. In Robert Warren's words (as quoted earlier), 'God's way of being human has been revealed in Jesus. It is available to us all through the Holy Spirit. It is being demonstrated in a church near you.'[1] That is a challenge to each and every church. We are called by God in the church to demonstrate the gospel, to demonstrate God's way of being human. It is a very different way of being human to the world's way, and so the church should be a very different community from the world. A church that was different in the seven ways described above would be different in the ways we are supposed to be different. Robert Warren's experience as the Church of England's National Officer for Evangelism led him to believe that the single most important factor in evangelism was a local church demonstrating the gospel.

* * *

Here are some examples of churches which are attempting to demonstrate the gospel by engaging with the world and its needs around them in a distinctive way.

Oak Tree Anglican Fellowship

Oak Tree is a second-generation church plant from Holy Trinity, Brompton, home of the Alpha course. Unusually, it was an initiative of the area bishop. Within this episcopal area was the London district of Acton, served by a total of some 23 churches of all denominations, including six Anglican parish churches, nearly all of which were small and declining. At the bishop's suggestion Mike Clarkson, an American ordained in the Church of England, and a group of about 50 others from the church of St Barnabas, West Kensington, were planted in Acton as the Oak Tree Anglican Fellowship in 1993.

---

1 Robert Warren, *Building Missionary Congregations* (Church House, 1995), p. 22.

At the beginning, the bishop's move was almost universally unpopular among the existing churches, not least the Anglican ones. Notwithstanding Oak Tree's declarations that it did not intend to steal other people's sheep, indeed that it wished to serve the other churches of the area, it was met with hostility and suspicion. The story of how God sovereignly overcame this hostility and of how Oak Tree became accepted in the area needs to be told for the glory of God. But it needs to be told by someone else at some other time. Here, we simply want to follow the development of Oak Tree's calling to be a church serving the other churches and the wider community of Acton.

Mike Clarkson was instrumental in drawing together a group of church leaders who recognised that the regeneration of the area and the establishment of God's kingdom in Acton were tasks beyond the resources of any of them, and that as churches they needed to work and pray together. This initiative produced a joint prayer meeting and a shared Alpha course supported by 14 of the area's churches. As the millennium approached, all the churches agreed to work together on a two-year project called Acton Initiative towards the Millennium (AIM).

AIM led to various combined efforts in the areas of youth work, mission and social action, and a bi-monthly newsletter to all churchgoers. Churches which had for years regarded one another with distaste or disdain discovered they could work side by side on such common projects, and even make friends with each other in the process. It was not a matter of achieving some sort of doctrinal or liturgical unity so that they could work together, but rather discovering that by working together for the kingdom of God they had a unity of purpose which transcended their doctrinal disagreements and different liturgical traditions.

As part of Acton's millennium celebrations, eleven of the churches combined to lay on a summer barbeque in a local park. For four days, 500 people a day were given a free lunch in the park with music, friendly conversation and a great atmosphere. A hundred and fifty church members were involved, providing food, cooking, serving and clearing up. Activities such as these did not pass unnoticed in the community at large, and led to an extraordinary proposition from the local borough council.

The borough of Ealing, in which Acton is situated, was preparing a bid for funding, both from central government and from the European Union, for a plan to regenerate some of Acton's poorest areas and estates under the Social Regeneration Initiative (SRI). Various local agencies were involved, but to be successful such an application had to involve partners with direct access to the people in the local communities which would be affected by the scheme. Consultation and communication between the institutions concerned and the people on the ground would be a vital condition for success in the initiative. The borough council turned to the Acton churches. Studies of the area had shown that there were many different subcommunities in Acton and the only common thread that ran through them all was the network of Acton churches. So the churches were invited to join the Action Acton project as partners providing the links with the diverse communities and groups in the area.

Mike Clarkson himself had grave reservations about the churches' ability to fulfil the expectations which the borough seemed to have. He was aware, as perhaps the council was not, that the churches were fragile, under-resourced, and not as unified as they might appear. There would also be questions at other levels about the political correctness of the churches' participation. Acton is a multi-ethnic, multi-faith area and, as Mike pointed out, the churches were Christian. Was it appropriate for the borough to involve a confessional organisation like the church in this way? But in the face of all objections the borough was adamant. No one else had links across the area, had people living in every street and tower block, had representatives in touch with the views and aspirations of local people – except the churches. And, miracle of miracles, the Acton churches were not perceived by the wider community as a handful of warring factions, but as one body. So, seeing this as the very hand of God, and with the further encouragement of the bishop, the churches agreed. As a result the churches of Acton are a constituent part of the New Hope Project, embracing more than 40 separate initiatives of urban regeneration. The present budget at their disposal is £47 million, with the prospect of a second and even larger tranche to come.

Here is the fruit of the church embracing its calling to be a distinct and distinctive community, not withdrawing from but reaching out into and engaging with the world around it in ways which demonstrate the grace of God. The opportunity of being involved in the spending of £47 million in an area of two square miles is not going to come to every church or even group of churches, but it is a faith-building example of what God can do when we are single-mindedly faithful to him and to our calling. The fact that Oak Tree was a nonparochial Anglican church, far from disqualifying it from such involvement with the community, actually made such involvement easier. Parochial boundaries tend to reduce our vision, to isolate us from other churches outside our own parishes, and to make us defensive and suspicious. It was Oak Tree's freedom from such a parochial outlook that allowed Mike Clarkson and other members of the church to explore and embrace new forms of co-operation and engagement.

* * *

Norwich Community Church

NCC is a new church, part of the New Frontiers International movement. Since its formation in 1986 the church has met in a variety of premises, including a suburban high school, a redundant medieval church within the ancient city walls, and a city-centre concert hall. Each move was made either as a result of numerical growth or out of a desire to engage more effectively with the city.

This church was one which was heavily impacted by the move of the Holy Spirit in 1994 which became known as 'the Toronto Blessing'. Perhaps contrary to most people's understanding of that spiritual movement, its main effect on NCC was to move the church out into new initiatives in social action. Having refurbished one redundant Anglican church as a worship centre, this church then took on another and converted it for outreach to the city's youth. With a cappuccino bar, a pool room and an auditorium for music and arts events, it also attracts young people through guitar classes and the facility to record their own music.

Then, in 1997, NCC had the opportunity to buy the former premises of Norwich Lads Club. The Lads Club had been a philanthropic venture stemming out of the First World War, now in a run-down area which had become the 'red light' district of the city. Other Christian initiatives were moving into the area, such as the Magdalene Group, an outreach to the prostitutes. In faith, NCC bought the large but dilapidated buildings of the Lads Club with the vision of creating not just a new and enlarged worship centre for themselves, but also a social centre serving the local community and helping to regenerate the whole area.

An extensive social survey carried out by professional consultants and funded by the city council enabled the church to identify specific needs which the new facilities could be designed to meet. This inner-city district badly needed the equivalent of a village hall – rooms which could be hired out for everything from housing association meetings to children's parties and barn dances. On a different scale, it appeared that big businesses would like to pay good money for the use of a large, high-quality conference centre for training their staff. The Lads Club had always provided facilities for sports, from rollerskating to boxing. The large arena which would become the main worship area on a Sunday could continue to be used for badminton and volleyball.

With redevelopment costs in excess of half a million pounds, help has been forthcoming for the community aspects of the project from government and local government sources, as well as other Christian and charitable trusts. But still, much of the money, including the initial purchase price of £123,000, has come and will come directly from the church members themselves. As the redevelopment has progressed many other activities and services have moved in: a baby and toddler group, adult literacy classes for dispersed asylum seekers, shower and laundry facilities for the homeless off the streets. A gym is being prepared, the use of which will be heavily discounted to local people unable to afford the fancy prices of city fitness centres. There are plans for gentle workouts for the over-sixties, relaxation classes and weight-reduction programmes which address the whole person, body, mind and spirit, music classes on Saturday mornings for local children as music is increasingly squeezed out of the budgets and curriculum time of local schools, debt counselling and chiropody.

This is another example of a church with a strong sense of its own distinctive values but an equally strong sense of God's call to be engaged with the local community. But it is an even more instructive example of a church's proactive relationship to buildings. A new church like this is light on its feet. As its requirements change, so, with a minimum of fuss, the church moves on. If a building outlives its utility, it is left behind. Nothing could be further from the culture of conservation, and churches tied to the maintenance of historic buildings for their own sake.

The supreme irony is that Norwich Community Church was allowed, even encouraged and asked, to redevelop redundant Anglican buildings in ways which, had they still been in use as parish churches, would have been absolutely unthinkable – in one case to make a modern worship centre, in the other a new youth centre. The moral of this is: let the old buildings fall into disrepair and abandon the forlorn attempt to keep them open for worship, and you will soon be able to do what you like with them, even worship in them again.

*   *   *

Fountain of Life

Our own church has tried to develop ways of living in the economy of grace. Twice a year, in spring and autumn, we organise a clothes swap. Everyone turns out their drawers and cupboards at home and brings clothes which for one reason or another they no longer want; maybe the children have grown out of them; maybe Mum has got fatter or thinner or simply would not be seen dead in last year's fashions (Dad may have got fatter or thinner too). It is not a jumble sale. Clothes that are shabby, faded, torn or worn out go for rags; we are only interested in good second-hand clothes. Neither does any money change hands; no one buys or sells. Everybody brings their clothes; they are laid on tables or hung on rails; then everyone takes their pick. It is great fun, even more fun than shopping, and, in a church where not a few families struggle to make ends meet, it is an effective way for those who have more to share with those who have less.

There are always vast quantities of clothes left over. Sometimes they are bagged up for the Salvation Army, sometimes they go off to be shipped abroad, sometimes other groups are offered the chance to share with us the goodness of God. In this way we seek to 'do good to all people, especially to those who belong to the family of believers' (Galatians 6:10).

A similar project is The Lord's Food Store. People in the congregation are invited to bring to church each Sunday one item of grocery, preferably nonperishable. These are put into

The Lord's Food Store and distributed each week to those in the congregation who are in need. It is not always easy to find out who the needy are; even in the church people are reluctant to talk about their financial problems. Need today does not take the form of children going without shoes, but is more likely to take the form of unmanageable debt, family budgets crippled by redundancy or the demands of the Child Support Agency, or just plain low pay. Such problems, of course, often need more long-term help and counselling, which we also try to provide, but The Lord's Food Store has proved a useful weapon for financial firefighting. Although the majority of recipients are members of the church, the food is available to other people, of whose bona-fide need we are assured, in the community at large.

Fountain of Life also runs a furniture store. We accept gifts of good second-hand furniture, subject to the current conditions of fire and electrical safety. We store these in our own premises until someone inside or outside the fellowship has a need, and then the necessary items are given away. We have members of the church who are qualified to test electrical goods and others who have trailers and vans for transportation. Again no money changes hands in any direction; no one buys or sells, everything is given. Those outside the church who receive items of furniture and household goods are left with a note which simply says:

FOUNTAIN OF LIFE FURNITURE STORE
Please accept these items as a free gift from
Fountain of Life Church
We believe that God loves you and wants to bless you.
We hope that you will see these items as a sign of his care for you.

In other ways, we try to reach out to the community more directly with signs of God's grace. Once a year we organise a Free Family Fun Day. At the local community centre we bring together a host of attractions for children and other members of the family: bouncy castles, mini-go-karting, bungee running, a circus workshop, face-painting, craft activities, croquet, hair-braiding, football and swingball competitions, entertainment from a barbershop quartet, barbeque, ice creams and refreshments. The only difference between this and a traditional church fête is that everything is free. Far from raising money for the church, the church pays the (considerable) bills, but everyone has a lot of fun together. Nobody *needs* a fun day like this, but, like so many of God's gifts to us, it is a sign of his grace.

At Christmas we were invited by the local supermarket to sing carols in the main entrance area one evening when the store stayed open for late shopping. As we sang carols to those who were coming and going, we also gave out parcels of sweets and cards from the church, wishing everyone a happy Christmas.

It is surprisingly difficult for many people to accept the idea of such free gifts. People at the supermarket tended to assume that if we were carol-singing there must be collecting boxes. What has the church done with God's free gift of his Son? Has it turned it into an excuse for fundraising? At the Family Fun Day children and adults repeatedly enquire, 'How much is it?' They are told over and over again, 'It's free, like the love of God.'

PART FIVE

Conclusion

13

Leadership Issues

Churches in missionary mode require a different type of leadership from churches in maintenance mode. Indeed, there is a sense in which churches in maintenance mode do not need and do not want 'leadership' at all. It is no coincidence that it is only in the last few years that it has become commonplace to talk about 'church leaders'. Leadership assumes some sort of motion; people who are not going anywhere do not need to be led. The style of leadership that suits a church in maintenance mode is essentially pastoral, whereas the style that is needed by a church in missionary mode is best defined as apostolic. David Pytches, in his book *Leadership for New Life*, identifies what is needed in a missionary situation as 'church leadership for breaking new ground for the Kingdom of God'.[1]

In a missionary situation the metaphors for the church's task are those of exploration and travel, of construction and development, of conflict and even battle. All these spheres of human activity are ones in which leadership is of prime importance. In these fields nothing is achieved by weak or incompetent leaders except muddle and confusion. In the Second World War the turning point in Britain came when Winston Churchill took

1 David Pytches, *Leadership for New Life* (Hodder & Stoughton, 1998), p. 19.

over as prime minister from Neville Chamberlain. The quality of leadership is no less important in the fields of industry and commerce. The fortunes of public companies are demonstrably related to the calibre of their leadership: Bill Gates and Microsoft, Anita Roddick and Body Shop are just two examples. The troubles of Laura Ashley and Marks and Spencer can be dated from the demise of their eponymous founders or their families. Leadership is all about vision and direction.

Churches accustomed to functioning for over a thousand years in maintenance mode are not generally paying sufficient attention to the importance of this quality of leadership. Most denominations select people for ordained or public ministry for their qualities or potential qualities as pastors and teachers. There may be a growing search for people with the qualities of evangelists, but few of the older churches seem to be looking or testing for the qualities of an apostle: someone who will lead a church in breaking new ground for the kingdom of God. Yet it is just as feasible to test potential candidates for qualities such as these; the army does it, and even industry does it on a routine basis.

A really successful organisation depends on the development and empowering of leadership gifts at every level. Some organisations achieve this better than others. In Britain one of our best models is the army. Whereas in most walks of life Britain has been steadily slipping down the league tables, the British army is still recognised as one of the best in the world. This has much to do with the army's ethos of encouraging and rewarding initiative and responsibility right through the ranks. The army requires both in its officers and its men discipline under authority and a willingness to think for themselves.

Much in the life of the contemporary church, however, not least the contemporary Church of England, breeds a very different ethos. Recent developments in the nature of the church as an organisation, the old conception of the clergy as a professional class and the consequent confusion in the present about their status and role, all militate against the development of a leadership that is breaking new ground for the kingdom of God.

In the last 40 years there have been two significant trends in the nature of the Church of England as an organisation: the incorporation of the church, and its democratisation. The marks of incorporation are centralisation, bureaucratisation and regulation. A glance at the growth of the diocesan office and its staff over the last 40 years tells the whole story. More and more decisions are made centrally, either in diocesan committees or in London. What such a church is looking for in its clergy is essentially apparatchiks: people who will grease the wheels and keep the machine running smoothly. The ideal country parson today is someone who can provide a skeleton programme of services in a mushrooming number of village churches, who will baptise, marry and bury the parishioners on demand, who raises the funds to pay the diocesan quota in full (very important, that one), who attends to the quinquennial repairs on the ancient buildings, who chairs the meetings, and who, above all, does not upset anyone. Such is the ideal company servant. But it does not break new ground for the kingdom of God.

Then there is the democratisation of the church. The general influence of the secular culture, the introduction of synodical government in 1970, and the more recent innovation of the stipend quota (an oblique system involving the payment of the clergy by the laity), have all led to an ethos of the rule of the majority in the church. In a democratic church the ideal leader is a person who can negotiate consensus, who can smooth over the differences, who can facilitate agreements and then get those agreements implemented. Such a leader sees all sides of the argument and then helps differing parties to discover common ground and common purpose. It is a model with which the hierarchy of the Church of England seems to identify very strongly – but it is not a scriptural pattern of leadership, and democracy is not a scriptural pattern of government in the church. The people of God are supposed to be governed by

God, not by the people. The church was never a democracy, either in the Old Testament or in the New. Neither Moses, nor David, nor Jesus took votes among their followers about what to do next. God does not give visions to committees, only to individual men and women. It may be appropriate to take counsel, to seek the confirmation or discernment of other believers, but the prophetic revelation that breaks new ground for the kingdom of God comes to individuals whom God raises up to be leaders. Such vision may be given to anyone in the church, to a new Christian as much as to a bishop or elder. The church needs to be able to recognise and respond to such vision however it arises.

Inherited patterns of ministry in the churches, not least in the Church of England, tend to discourage such openness. The Victorian understanding of the clergy as professional people,[2] comparable to doctors or lawyers, has cast a blight over what is patronisingly called 'the laity'. In those terms 'lay' leaders can be seen at best as unwashed, untrained amateurs who fill the gaps or act as inadequate substitutes for the great men themselves – monkeys standing in for the organ-grinder. This is how too many people, among both the clergy and the laity, still see 'lay ministry'.

The exigencies of the decline in the numbers of clergy and in the resources to pay them have led to the development of many new forms of nonstipendiary clerical ministry and lay ministry in all the churches – developments which have left the old 'professional' clergy feeling anxious and confused about their role. The clergy have recently been responding to this anxiety by redefining their role in terms of trainers or enablers of others in the church. But the clergy face two dilemmas in encouraging the leadership gifts of others, because a measure of trust and delegation is involved, and there are always risks involved in delegation. The first is that the person to whom a task is dele-

2 See Anthony Russell, *The Clerical Profession* (SPCK, 1980).

gated may not do it as well as the established leader does it, or may even prove unable to do it at all. The second is that the person to whom the task is delegated may do it better than the established leader does it. In the first case, it seems quicker and easier to continue to do the thing ourselves. In the second, are we not in danger of making ourselves redundant? It is a confident leader indeed who can enjoy his subordinates outperforming him. In any case, this is only a perpetuation of the model of monkeys and organ-grinders: now the organ-grinders are not just there to grind organs, but to teach the monkeys to be mini-organ-grinders. That enables the organ-grinders to go on thinking of themselves as organ-grinders and of the monkeys as monkeys, but it does not alter the paradigm in the church.

This clerical anxiety has its roots in a deficiency in the categories available to us to define our role. The first category we lack is that of leadership; the second is that of authority and discipline. One of the fruits of the charismatic renewal has been a recovery of the biblical understanding of every-member or whole-body ministry. According to Paul's exposition in 1 Corinthians 12 and elsewhere, *every* member of the church is given gifts by the Holy Spirit for the common good of the body of Christ. The Bible knows nothing of our distinction between clergy and laity. Traditional patterns of church life with a professional clergy have encouraged everyone to think of the church as a cruise-liner: a ship on which most of the people are passengers, enjoying the ride or complaining as the case may be, expecting to be suitably entertained and waited on by the crew. Paul's idea of the church in these terms would be much more that of a battleship, on which there are no passengers, but every person aboard is a member of the crew with a vital function to perform. For the ship to work and fight effectively, each person has to fulfil his or her own role as professionally as the next, but one of the people on board has to be the captain. It is the captain's role which we need to understand in relation to the life of the church.

The captain is the leader of the ship; his distinctive role is to exercise authority. Obviously the captain is not the person who does everything on the ship. Neither is the captain the person who trains everyone to do everything on the ship. The captain is the person who ensures that everything everyone does on the ship is co-ordinated; he makes the strategic decisions about which course the ship is to steer and about its conduct in action; he looks after the *esprit de corps* and when necessary exerts discipline. It is unlikely that the captain is as good a cook as the chef in the galley – indeed, he may not be able to cook at all; the captain is also unlikely to be an engineer or mechanic capable of maintaining the engines. He is therefore not equipped to do those jobs, nor to train members of his crew in their particular skills, but that does not mean he is redundant. His role is to be the captain and he is in authority on the ship.

This is the thinking we need to understand in terms of the role of leaders in the church: leadership is a separate charism or grace, given by God and recognised by the church, and its function is to make the church an effective instrument for breaking new ground for the kingdom of God. Leadership is not a concept that can be reduced to something else. It is a separate and necessary function in the body of Christ.

Nonetheless, this charism of leadership is not one to be exercised by the captain of the ship alone. In a good navy, as in a good army, each person needs to be encouraged to develop qualities of leadership within the limits of his or her own sphere or role within the body. It is a vital part of the local church leader's job to develop the gifts and ministries of the various members of the body of Christ, to co-ordinate their functions, and to train up new leaders. It should be sheer joy for a church leader to discover and develop the gifting of a new youth worker or worship leader within the church. In the end the best and only way to develop such gifts is to give people the opportunity to practise them, to lead a youth group or to lead worship. There are training courses which can help; there are ways of practising skills in controlled situations; but in the end there is no substitute for hands-on experience. People learn to exercise the ministry of healing, not so much by being taught about it, but by laying hands on the sick and praying for them or commanding them to recover in Jesus' name.

In such development of gifts people need both freedom and supervision, and there is a subtle balance to be sought between the two. A horse needs to be ridden on a rein which is neither too tight nor too loose. If the rein is too tight the horse will fret and chafe against the bit and respond reluctantly to its rider's instructions. If the rein is too loose the horse will become self-willed and undisciplined and refuse to respond to the rider's wishes at all. It is the same with developing people's giftings in the church. A church leader who is constantly looking over someone's shoulder and checking up will create a sense of distrust and inferiority; a church leader who never enquires how things are going will cause people to lose heart and risks some real disaster. Like riding a horse, it can be an exciting and scary experience.

The same thing is true of developing the gift of leadership itself in others. The church desperately needs more good leaders, both for declining churches to thrive and for thriving churches to grow. The best way to recognise potential new leaders in the church is to notice who comes up with new ideas for the church, who can motivate others in putting those ideas into practice, and who has the perseverance to see a project through. Potential leaders often feel like a pain to the established leadership of the church. The only way to get rid of the pain is to give them enough rope either to prove themselves or to hang themselves. The whole church needs to be aware that these processes are going on all the time, that people can try out their gifts and ministries, that they are free to make mistakes, that they will be forgiven and loved and encouraged to do better. But within this framework of freedom and encouragement there needs also to be the security of knowing that someone is in control, that growth and experiment are under the authority of the appointed leaders, and that there is a ministry of correction and discipline. It is very much like the life of a healthy family, in which the children are encouraged to discover their gifts and potentiality and explore a measure of freedom, within the boundaries set by their parents and under their loving care. This is the leader, not so much as captain, but as father.

*   *   *

The supreme example of leadership in the church is, of course, the Lord Jesus. To explore some of these issues further, I want to take a passage of Scripture which reveals Jesus as leader and deals with questions of leadership in the church: Mark 10:32–45.

[32] They were on their way up to Jerusalem, with Jesus leading the way, and the disciples were astonished, while those who followed were afraid. Again he took the Twelve aside and told them what was going to happen to him. [33] 'We are going up to Jerusalem,' he said, 'and the Son of Man will be betrayed to the chief priests and teachers of the law. They will condemn him to death and will hand him over to the Gentiles, [34] who will mock him and spit on him, flog him and kill him. Three days later he will rise.'

[35] Then James and John, the sons of Zebedee, came to him. 'Teacher,' they said, 'we want you to do for us whatever we ask.'

[36] 'What do you want me to do for you?' he asked.

[37] They replied, 'Let one of us sit at your right and the other at your left in your glory.'

[38] 'You don't know what you are asking,' Jesus said. 'Can you drink the cup I drink or be baptised with the baptism I am baptised with?'

[39] 'We can,' they answered.

Jesus said to them, 'You will drink the cup I drink and be baptised with the baptism I am baptised with, [40] but to sit at my right or left is not for me to grant. These places belong to those for whom they have been prepared.'

[41] When the ten heard about this, they became indignant with James and John. [42] Jesus called them together and said, 'You know that those who are regarded as rulers of the Gentiles lord it over them, and their high officials exercise authority over them. [43] Not so with you. Instead, whoever wants to become great among you must be your servant, [44] and whoever wants to be first must be slave of all. [45] For even the Son of Man did not come to be served, but to serve, and to give his life as a ransom for many.'

First of all, Jesus teaches us in this passage what Christian leadership is not, and how it differs from worldly models of leadership. James and John entertain the idea that leadership is a matter of glory and status (v. 37). Earthly leaders too often see leadership as a matter of power and control (v. 42). Over against these ideas Jesus teaches, and by his life demonstrates, that kingdom leadership involves suffering and sacrifice (vv. 34, 38, 45), that kingdom leadership is a form of service. This last concept, however, is one which is easily misunderstood.

Leadership as service is sometimes interpreted as if it means submission. That is not what Jesus means. The only one to whom Jesus was in submission was his Father in heaven; he was not at the beck and call of anyone else. He was not at the disposal of the people of Capernaum, however great their needs might be (Mark 1:35–39). He was not at the beck and call of his own family (Mark 3:31–35). He would not be rebuked by Peter (Mark 8:32–33), and he would not gratify James and John (Mark 10:40). If Jesus submitted himself to the high priest and to Pontius Pilate at the end, it was his own decision to do so, in obedience to the Father (Mark 14:36). On one occasion he took a towel and washed his disciples' feet. This was the exception, not the rule; it only made the impression it did because Jesus did not normally do it. He did it on his own initiative, not at the demand of the disciples. A kingdom leader is not a doormat.

Leadership is indeed a service to the body of Christ, but it is the service of leadership. The church needs leaders, just as

Israel needed leaders. Deborah praised the Lord when the nation's leaders took the lead and the people followed willingly (Judges 5:2). If the appointed leaders in the church are not taking the lead, then either the church is leaderless or there are other unappointed leaders in the church who are leading it instead. A leaderless church will be going nowhere and, like any leaderless group, will quickly become dispirited. On the other hand, few groups remain completely leaderless for long; for better or worse, if the authorised leaders have abdicated their responsibility to lead, other unauthorised and unrecognised people will usually emerge to fill the vacuum. That is a recipe for internal power struggles and internecine fighting. The church needs leaders who will perform the service of leading.

We see in this passage more positive lessons about the nature of kingdom leadership. First, the leader is the one who decides on the direction in which the church is to go. Jesus said to them, 'We are going up to Jerusalem' (v. 33). This was a momentous decision, and certainly not the result of any committee meeting or democratic vote. Had they been asked for their opinion, the disciples, either out of incomprehension or fear, would certainly have voted against the proposition (v. 32). This is another way of saying that the leader is the person with the vision, and his service to the church is to be the keeper of the vision, the one who keeps the vision before the church. A good church leader, not being Jesus himself, and therefore not being infallible, will listen, not only to God from whom the vision must come, but also to other members of the church, especially other leaders and other prophetic people. But the leader cannot ultimately abdicate the responsibility for making decisions: the buck stops with him.

There is more to leadership than simply making decisions, however. The second positive lesson is that a leader can be recognised by the fact that he or she has followers. An old Chinese proverb says, 'A leader without followers is simply someone taking a walk.' Jesus set out to go up to Jerusalem and the disciples, in spite of their astonishment and fear, followed him (v. 32). Unlike the rulers of the Gentiles, Jesus could not compel anyone to follow him anywhere. Church leaders are in the same position. A good church leader is one who not only has a vision, but who also has followers. The ability to communicate vision to others and to inspire others to follow is part of the charism, gift or grace of leadership. It is partly that the vision, if it is truly from God in the first place, is self-authenticating – it carries its own authority. But it is also a calling from God to lead and the anointing of the Holy Spirit on the leader, which causes others to follow.

The third dimension of Christian leadership which we see from the example of Jesus is the willingness to go first, to lead from the front (v. 32). The Twelve would not have gone up to Jerusalem this time if Jesus had said to them, 'You go up to this Feast, I will come up later,' as he had said on a previous occasion (John 7:8). Jesus had to lead the way. During the First World War the highest casualty rates were sustained among the junior officers, the captains and lieutenants. It was their duty to go over the top of the trenches first. When the order came to attack, the junior officers had to climb the ladders, blow the whistle and call the men to follow them. If the officers had not gone first, the men would never have gone at all. That is leadership.

A golden rule for leaders is never to ask other people to do what you are not prepared to do yourself. It may be washing people's feet; it may be facing up to angry opponents. If the church is breaking new ground for the kingdom of God, there will certainly be opposition. Ground can only be taken for the kingdom of God if it is taken from the kingdom of the enemy. It is the leader's calling to draw the enemy's fire to himself first of all. He is the shepherd who must stand between the sheep and the wolf. That is why the service of a Christian leader is not about power and glory, but about suffering and sacrifice (v. 45).

It remains to enquire where the vision comes from and how

it is received by the Christian leader in the church. It goes without saying that vision must come from God if it is to be fruitful
for his kingdom. There is a vital difference, which every church
leader has to learn, between good ideas and God's ideas. There
is no shortage of good ideas for the church – indeed, there is a
bewildering multitude of them. But any congregation can only
move forward one step at a time, and there is no substitute for
hearing from God what that next step should be. Vision, then,
means having some long-term, macro vision of the goal or des-
tination of the journey, and also a series of short-term, micro
visions of the steps necessary to advance the church in the right
direction.

The primary source of vision for the church leader must
always be the Bible. The Bible contains the canon of Scripture.
'Canon' means a rule or standard of measurement. The Bible is
the rule or standard against which we have always to measure
the church's faith, the Christian's manner of life, and the life of
the church itself. The primary source of Jesus' own vision was
the Old Testament Scriptures. In the parallel passage to Mark
10:32–45 in Luke's Gospel, Jesus says, 'We are going up to
Jerusalem, and everything that is written by the prophets about
the Son of Man will be fulfilled. He will be turned over to the
Gentiles. They will mock him, insult him, spit on him, flog him
and kill him. On the third day he will rise again' (Luke
18:31–33). This makes it clear that Jesus' own understanding of
the way which God had prepared for him was derived from
meditation on the Scriptures.

A very useful exercise for a church leader or any church
group is to compare the descriptions we have in the New
Testament of the life of the apostolic church with the reality of
church life today. The contrast is salutary. The temptation is to
rationalise the alarming discrepancies, so that we can feel more
comfortable about the place where we are. The challenge is to
set out to bring our own experience of the church into conformity with the rule or standard we have been given in Scripture.
It is this constant, serious submission of ourselves and our

churches to the God-given model of the New Testament which will provide and renew our macro vision of where the church ought to be.

As to the steps by which we get from where we are to where we ought to be, the second source of inspiration in Jesus' life is his attention to what the Father was doing. 'I tell you the truth,' Jesus said, 'the Son can do nothing by himself; he can do only what he sees his Father doing, because whatever the Father does the Son also does' (John 5:19). The church leader's job is to see what God is doing and to do it with him. Certainly, if he is invited to do so, God will be at work in every church and neighbourhood. Too often in the church we devise our own plans and strategies and then ask God to bless them. It is much more fruitful to discern what God's plans are, and then for us to bless and co-operate with those.

We can begin to discern what the Father is doing by looking around at other churches. Where are the churches that are growing? Where and how are people being converted? Where are there signs and wonders which confirm the truth of the Word? God is in the business of glorifying his name and Jesus is in the business of building his church, so where we see these things taking place we can see that the Spirit is at work. Church leaders should not be afraid to look at successful growing churches and ask how they are doing it and what is working for them. There is no point in going on doing things which are simply no longer working, which are not producing the fruit of changed lives. Where lives are being changed, God is at work. Let us find out how he is doing it, and what methods or tools he is using today.

By such investigation and research we will be able to see what the Father is doing in a general way, in the context of the time and culture in which we have to operate. We also need, however, to be able to see more specifically what he is doing in our own situation. It may be no more than a question of timing for our own local church. Alpha is obviously one way in which God is at work, but so are Willow Creek-type seeker services and Kidz Klub. Cell church values are obviously important, but so is church-planting. Mentoring may be producing mature Christians, but we also need to be affecting the secular world in which we live. Which of the many batons lying around does God want us to pick up and run with?

Jesus was able to read the signs of the times, to know the right time for the next step. On many occasions before the final journey up to Jerusalem the Jews had tried to arrest or to kill Jesus, but up until now Jesus had evaded them: his time had not yet come (John 7:30; 8:20; 10:39). But then the times changed and he set his face steadfastly towards Jerusalem, knowing what awaited him there. His hour had come (John 12:23). We need to learn to see what God is doing at a particular time and in each particular situation.

This is not a matter of making things happen, but of noticing what is happening already. The development of the Alpha course itself offers an object lesson. At the beginning, the Alpha course was devised as a response to something that was already happening: people were becoming Christians at the church of Holy Trinity, Brompton, and they needed a course of instruction in the basic elements of Christian faith and practice. After a while, the staff noticed that the people taking the course were not all new Christians; some were not Christians at all, but were enquiring more generally about the meaning of life and wondering if Christianity had any answers. At that point the focus of the course changed to make it more open and inviting for people outside the church altogether.

The next step came when Alpha course staff at HTB noticed that people were travelling extraordinary distances to attend: not just across London or from the Home Counties, but commuting from places as far away as Liverpool and York. It looked as if God was thinking bigger than Kensington. So, in 1993, HTB offered the first national Alpha conference to teach other churches the principles and practices of Alpha. From then on, the invitations to run Alpha conferences in other parts of Britain and eventually all over the world began to flood in.

Alpha as a worldwide phenomenon did not arise out of some global vision or megalomania, but simply out of one local church seeing what the Father was doing and doing it with him.

*   *   *

God is not going to use each local church in such a far-reaching way, but each church leader can learn the same gift of seeing what God is doing and doing it with him. It means noticing the small things that God is doing, the straws in the wind. It means being able to set aside our own agendas or preconceptions of what God ought to be doing and searching for God's fingerprints in the church and the world around us. It means dealing with the situations and the issues that actually arise, whether we want them to or not, and working with rather than against the grain of events. It means being willing, even in leadership, to make mistakes and backtrack sometimes, rather than blunder on stubbornly when it is obvious that God is not with us. It is not easy; it is leadership.

14

Building a New Church Alongside the Old

I have been ordained in the Church of England for over 35 years, long enough to understand the problems of change in such a large and old institution. Back in the days when people, including myself, still believed that Christian unity could be brought about by committees and schemes, I prepared a paper on 'ecumenical geography' in the region where I lived. I did this in co-operation with all the major denominations in the area and with various ecumenical bodies. The paper drew attention to the problems for ecumenical co-operation caused by the fact that all the denominations work within their own separate sets of geographical boundaries. It is often such practical, nontheological factors which inhibit working together and talking together, as much as great doctrinal differences. I finished by outlining the sort of modest changes that would be needed to facilitate ecumenical co-operation at various levels.

Needless to say, nothing ever happened. Nobody disagreed with what I had written, but nobody did anything about it. For me, it was a defining moment, an experience that changed my expectations and helped to alter the direction of my life. Through that episode, I realised the nature and dimensions of institutional inertia. The more democratised an institution has become (and all the churches, with the possible exception of the Roman Catholic Church, have become heavily democratised), the more the church is governed by committees and synods and is committed to processes of consultation, the greater the inertia that has been built into the system. It is not just that change is very difficult to bring about, but that the sheer cost of bringing the change about, in terms of time and effort, is out of all proportion to the benefits the change might actually produce.

I can see now that the time and effort that would have been required to bring about the modest and sensible boundary changes that I proposed would simply have been another massive distraction from the much more urgent and significant task of making disciples in our nation. I am profoundly grateful, now, that my bright ideas fell on deaf ears. I only wish that those ears had been more open, then and now, to the God-given imperatives of the gospel and less open merely to the other distractions of denominational survival. The point is that, if we are waiting for the institutions of the church to change before we do the works of the kingdom, we shall wait for ever.

If you are a church leader and you think that if only you exercise enough love and patience your traditional congregation will eventually embrace a mission agenda, dream on. If you are a renewed Christian sitting in the pews of a traditional church and you think that if only you exercise enough love and patience the vicar will eventually be born again and filled with the Holy Spirit, dream on. If you are a congregation who want to turn your medieval architectural gem into a twenty-first-century worship centre, and you think that if only you take enough care to discuss your plans with everyone in sight and consult all the relevant authorities you will eventually be able to reorder your premises, dream on. Of course, there are occasional examples of all these miracles happening, which is why so many people do dream on. But the fact is that there are many more examples in which leaders, people and congregations are disappointed, frustrated, disillusioned and in despair in the face of the immovable blockages of institutional inertia.

And while everyone waits and prays, and exercises love and patience, the mission agenda continues to be neglected, the church continues to decline, and the nation goes from bad to worse.

Christians in a traditional church, leaders and people, have to realise that there are many people in the church or connected with the church, especially a parish church and especially a country parish church, for whom the church is a focus for a very different agenda from that of the kingdom of God. For some, the agenda is playing the organ and singing in the choir; for others, it is ringing the bells; for others, it is arranging the flowers; for others, it is history and architecture; for others, many others, it is the life of the village itself. Many people inside and outside the church want the village church to be a focus of unity in the village, something that brings people together and creates a sort of genial illusion that all is well. In such a situation a kingdom church which starts with the understanding that all is not well, and that God has come to do something about it, is a divisive and disturbing influence. But that is the only way that the church can be redeemed from irrelevance and ineffectuality. And time is short.

Many people today would tell us that the time is short until the Lord comes again. I have no personal revelation from God that this is so, but it may be. I am sufficiently historically aware to know that in many previous generations Christians have also believed that they lived in the days immediately preceding the return of the Lord, and that the signs of the end were manifest in their world. Just because others have been mistaken before, however, does not mean that this is not the time for the Lord to return now. Perhaps it is. But even if it is not, in other, more mundane, ways time is short.

People are dying all the time. Are they dying into a God-filled or a God-less eternity? The time in which we can change our minds, repent and believe the gospel is short. What are we, the Christians, the church, doing to reach people with the gospel before it is too late?

Even in their lives in this world, millions of our fellow countrymen and women are messing up the one chance we are given to find happiness and fulfilment. Drugs, addictions, debt, divorce, abuse are ruining lives even while I write and you read. What are we, the Christians, the church, doing to bring redemption and healing to broken and hurting human beings? Time is short, the labourers are few, the task is urgent. We have lost too much time already, we have lost too many generations, we cannot wait while the institutions change.

So, what are the options? The first is obviously to do what many people have done over the last 30 years: leave the old denominations and start again. It is ironic that the twentieth century, which many hoped would see the reunion of the older churches, ended by seeing the creation of many new ones. Nevertheless, the new churches have set forward the kingdom of God by clearing the decks and starting again with a biblical and apostolic agenda. Those of us in the older mainline churches should honour them and learn from them.

For many people there seems to be no alternative to leaving the older churches except staying and submitting to the bondages of old institutions, old buildings and old traditions – institutions, buildings and traditions which have manifestly failed to advance the mission of the church and the kingdom of God for at least a hundred years. The structural obstacles to change and renewal that we have explored in this book are immense: the legacy of Christendom, the parish system, and the heritage of ancient buildings. These are the bondages from which God's people must break free if they are to find the liberty to worship and serve Jesus alone.

I believe there is an alternative strategy that those in the older denominations can adopt: to build a new church alongside the old one.

The first element in this strategy is to leave the old church alone. Let the old congregation in the old building go on maintaining the old traditions. Threatening them with the new ways, or the renewed ways, of intimacy in worship, of ministry in the power of the Holy Spirit, of engaging with modern culture (which is about as alien to the old one as the culture of Outer Mongolia), is going to provoke anger and resentment and create a situation of conflict which blesses no one inside or outside the church. I have been there and done it, and I do not recommend it. When all is said and done, there is a validity in the old things and the old ways: they still mediate God to some people, particularly among the older generation. Any strategy for renewal should allow people to keep what is of value to them and nourishes their spiritual life, be it hymns, prayer books or pews.

There are 'old' churches which are full and flourishing; many of our ancient cathedrals with their formal liturgies and choirs are 'growing churches'. These congregations, like most significant churches today, are eclectic, drawing people in from a wide area for all the reasons which we have explored earlier. They tend to bear out the main thesis that I have advanced about mobility and viability; they are not functioning as parish churches in the proper sense of the word, even where that is what they technically are. But there must be a continuing place in the church, especially an inclusive national church like the Church of England, for a spirituality which has served so many for so long. The challenge is to find a new way and a new place for God to do a new thing alongside the old one.

The next element in the strategy is therefore to create new expressions of church. If we are to do this within our old denominations there are three key issues to consider: location, initiation and permission. Such new expressions of church should be radical from the beginning. Finding a new time, a gap in the existing Sunday or weekday programme, but using the old premises, seems an easier option at first, but alternative services in the old building, on the old territory, within the old institutional structures, are still likely to be the seedbeds of conflict in the future. A far-sighted strategy should foresee and forestall that conflict. A new place is more important than a new time. The constitution of the Church of England in particular is so dominated by geography and buildings that the only way to create true freedom is to find new places to meet and new places to worship. Place is a key issue, especially for Anglicans.

A new expression of church needs to start with an open mind about where it gathers as well as about how it worships and what it does. It is best to start by looking for a place to build, buy or borrow that will most fully meet the new church's needs. It is most unlikely, in the countryside at least, that this will be the medieval parish church. Perhaps a new expression of church should not be entirely closed to the possibility of using an old church building, but the presumption must be that another building in the area – a hall, a community centre, a school, a large house, an old chapel, a disused barn or warehouse – will make a more suitable worship and mission centre for the twenty-first century. At the beginning the new congregation will probably be better off hiring or borrowing rather than building or buying. As the church grows, its needs will change. A new church, unlike the old one, should be quick on its feet, able to move and grow without too much hassle.

It is neither necessary nor desirable to build such a new church alongside every old one. In the 1990s there was a push to plant new churches, with a goal of a mission-orientated church for every 1,000 people in the land. In the urban and suburban areas of Britain this might have seemed an inspiring idea, although the target was not reached in the 1990s. In the countryside, however, we face a different problem: we already have many more churches than we need to serve the existing churchgoing population, or even the potential churchgoing population. These are rarely mission-orientated churches, but there is no point in over-providing the countryside with new expressions of church just because it is already over-provided with old ones. We live in the age of the motor car. People travel. There is a horizon for daily domestic journeys, but it is much wider than the individual parish. How far will people travel to take the children to music lessons or riding lessons? How far will people travel to the golf club or the bowls club?

That is the sort of distance that people can be expected to travel to church. If there were a new expression of church within ten miles of everyone in the countryside, that would probably be a sensible place to start. One viable church will do more for the kingdom of God than ten nonviable ones.

The next key issue is initiation. The issues of initiation and permission have to be seen together. In most of the older denominations there is an authority structure which either gives or withholds permission for new adventures in faith. In the Church of England those who can give or withhold permission are local clergy and bishops. But that does not mean that the permission-givers have to be the people who take the initiative. In fact, the initiative for new expressions of church can come from any level. In the Church of England the bishop can take the initiative, as in the case of Oak Tree Anglican Fellowship in Acton. The local clergy can take the initiative, as in the case of The Carpenter's Arms in Deal. Or the initiative can come from a group of ordinary people who see the need to establish a new expression of church in the area. This was more the case with the original Soul Survivor youth congregation in Watford, which was initiated and is still led by an unordained youth worker, Mike Pilavachi.

Such is the level of alarm in the old institutional church at the continuing failure of the old ways, that there is a new openness among many permission-givers to new initiatives from the grass roots, an openness which probably did not exist 20 or even ten years ago.

The establishment of such new expressions of church involves a process of negotiation between the group of people, of whatever age, who will form the nucleus of the new congregation, and the various permission-givers. There will have to be negotiation over issues of leadership and accountability, of the relationship of the new church to the old ones round about, and of this new expression of Christianity to the old structures. With a measure of trust and goodwill these issues, as we have seen, are not incapable of resolution.

Such is the nature and weight of institutional inertia, however, that the development of new expressions of church must often precede, rather than follow, such negotiations. Old institutions like the Church of England are almost incapable of radical innovation themselves. The Anglican way of life is much more typically to respond to and allow things which are already being done – *faits accomplis*. Historical examples of this are simply too numerous to mention: just about every change in Anglican worship over the last 150 years has been the result of people doing things first and obtaining permission afterwards. It is not a risk-free strategy, but the worst that can happen is that the new initiative ends up outside the old denomination instead of inside it, and there is life beyond the old denominations.

Some will say that such new expressions of church in a country town or village will be divisive. In one sense, of course, they will. But it sounds a whole lot better if we talk about diversity instead of division. In spite of the Act of Uniformity, the Church of England has lived with diversity for centuries, and has even prided itself on its ability to contain and embrace diversity. For 150 years the Church of England has been high church in one place, low church in another, and broad church in another. Why can we not add another element of cultural and spiritual diversity by giving permission for new expressions of church alongside the old ones?

If there is one thing that my generation should have learned about Christian unity, it is that unity is more a matter of the mind and will than a matter of structures and committees. By aiming at Christian unity as an end in itself, the twentieth century failed to achieve it. We discover unity between churches and congregations when we cease to concentrate on the church and start to concentrate on the kingdom of God. We find that we can live and work side by side with Christians of other traditions and denominations if we are all focused on the extension of the kingdom of God and doing the kingdom things that Jesus called us all to do.

There are always going to be temptations to jealousy and anxiety, especially among church leaders. But if our focus is on the kingdom of God, where it ought to be, we should be able to rejoice at the growth and prosperity of other manifestations of the church as well as our own. It is, after all, God's church in all its manifestations, not ours. One of the marks of the charismatic renewal and one of the authentications that this is truly a work of God's Spirit is the measure of spiritual unity that exists between renewed churches of all denominations and streams. For charismatic Christians, the question of whether one is a Baptist, another an Anglican, another a Pentecostal, another new church, is rarely of primary significance; the only question that really matters is whether a person is a Christian or not.

Life is simply too short and the kingdom of God is too urgent to waste time on elaborate schemes to change the structures. I do not expect to see the parish system or the constitutional establishment of the Church of England abolished in my lifetime. The church will go on tinkering with its structures and its constitution, but I doubt if it will change rapidly. Too many people in the church still believe in the parish system and too many people are still in love with the old buildings for a sudden revolution to take place. The old structures may slowly collapse under their own weight, but people will still treasure the ruins. Meanwhile, for the sake of the kingdom of God, we must press on regardless with the real work: the renewal of the church, the reconversion of the nation, and the healing and salvation of bodies and souls. The change from one agenda to another, from maintenance to mission, and the change from one culture to another, from, let us say, Victorian to postmodern, are so difficult to manage that the aim of our strategy should be to reduce to a minimum the conflict and pain, while not compromising the integrity and imperatives of the gospel.

*   *   *

Forty years ago God called me to be a missionary. I have spent the intervening years trying to discover what that call meant for me, and where and how it was to be fulfilled. Somewhat to my surprise, I was drawn into the English countryside and God has been teaching me about being a missionary there ever since.

My earliest lessons were simply lessons in my own ineffectuality and the ineffectiveness of the church. In a positive sense it was a process of disillusionment, of seeing through the illusions that populate the countryside, the siren calls of the past that lead the missionary astray. It is progress of a sort to recognise that the emperor does not in fact have any clothes. When I was sufficiently convinced of my own ineffectuality, I was ready to learn more about the power of God, and I was baptised in the Holy Spirit in 1983. Soon after that God took me out of parish ministry for four years, during which time he re-educated me theologically and retrained me for ministry, in ways of which my theological college in the 1960s had not dreamed.

When I became again the rector of two country villages in 1988, I set out to do and teach the new things I had learned about the kingdom of God. God worked with me and confirmed the word with signs following. No doubt there were ways in which I could have done it all better, but I do not repent of the enterprise, because it was nothing less than that of creating a church which would be an effective agent of mission. The aim of the missionary must be to create a missionary church.

I do not believe that the issues we have faced and with which we have all struggled these last 15 years are trivial ones or significant to our locality alone. We are living through a season of change for the church in Europe greater than any in the past 1,000 years. An old order is coming to an end. It is our present task, not least in the countryside, to help a new order to emerge.

After several years of trying to change the old into the new, I came to a conclusion that I formulated in this way: it is better to build a new church alongside the old one. At the time I meant that it was better to grow a new congregation, a congregation of new Christians or renewed Christians, alongside the old congregation. But God, I have discovered, often takes us at our word more literally than we expect. I have ended up not only growing a new congregation, but actually building a new church in the same village as the old one. I did not plan or foresee such an outcome. It is the result of confronting not just the personal obstacles or the congregational obstacles, but also the structural obstacles to renewal. The renewal of the church and its mission involves much more than we thought: it involves, in the end, the renewal of the structures themselves.

Postscript

From the point of view of someone working in a local church, what I have said in this book is the best advice I can give about the way forward, and I personally have given up any attempt to change the church at any other level than that. I am aware, however, that there are people who share these concerns at a national level and who may be able to bring about change, albeit slow and piecemeal. So it may be worth adding one more voice to that process.

Repentance comes before amendment of life, and repentance means changing the mind. Before structural changes, there must be spiritual changes, as well as changes in the way we think and in our values. These are the crucial changes, and if these changes take place then the structural changes are not so difficult to see or to make. The fundamental change is in the way we perceive the church in relation to society and the world around us. We have to be delivered from the mentality of Christendom, from the fantasy of a Christian society. We do not live in one now, and neither should we expect to live in one before the end of the age. Christians may aspire to influence society, but should not aspire to rule it. The kingdom of God is not of this world.

If we grasp that, then we shall grasp that we live permanently in a missionary situation. Our efforts will then be directed towards making disciples for Christ and leavening the social lump, tasks which will continuously engage us until the Lord returns. At both of these things we could, by the grace and power of God and in co-operation with Christian brothers and sisters in all the churches, be spectacularly successful – if we gave up the illusion of a mission already accomplished.

The Church of England, especially in the countryside, faces a particular problem with its responsibility for ancient buildings. A way must be found of handing this responsibility over to those whose primary love and calling is to look after the national inheritance (perhaps English Heritage); it is not the function of the Church of Jesus Christ to do so. The present responsibility causes a major and fatal distortion in the life of the people of God. If the strategy of the church was formed by its missionary calling and freed from the control of buildings, it would be possible to see more clearly what we ought to be doing, the best way of doing it, and the buildings we actually need to do it in. Meanwhile, let us adopt a policy of 'as if . . .': we should plan and act *as if* we were not responsible for all these ancient monuments, and see what happens.

I believe that the key concept in any wider missionary strategy is the concept of *viability*. Strong centres of spiritual life need to be nurtured and reinforced by diocesan policy, not used as milch cows to support lost causes. These strong centres will reproduce and multiply by themselves if they are given the freedom to do so; the land, even the countryside, can be recolonised for the kingdom of God if the colonists are not constrained by the parish system. The grip of the parish system needs at least to be loosened to allow new initiatives and church plants.

It is not for me or for bishops or for anyone else to prescribe where such strong centres of spiritual life should exist or develop; they may not always be where we expect or want them. We should start from where they are, not from where we think they ought to be. If God blesses and multiplies a church in Kensington, let us bless what he is doing. If God blesses and multiplies a church in downtown Sheffield, let us bless what he is doing. If God blesses and multiplies a church in the depths of the countryside, let us bless what he is doing. Nor is it for us to decide what sort of Christian spirituality such strong centres should enjoy. That is also God's prerogative. If God blesses and multiplies a Catholic church, let us bless what he is doing. If God blesses and multiplies a conservative evangelical church, let us bless what he is doing. If God blesses and multiplies a charismatic or Pentecostal church, let us bless what he is doing. Our job is not to prescribe what God should do or where he should do it, but to discern what God is doing and do it with him. At the moment we spend too much of our time, our money and our resources of people on doing things that God is manifestly not doing. How much more exciting and rewarding church life would be for all of us if we turned round and tried to do it God's way.

A Theology of the Baptism of the Holy Spirit

> It is very meet, right and our bounden duty, that we should at all times and in all places give thanks unto thee, O Lord, Holy Father, Almighty, Everlasting God, because thou didst give Jesus Christ thine only Son to be born as at this time for us; who by the operation of the Holy Ghost was made very man of the substance of the Virgin Mary his mother. (Preface for Christmas Day, Holy Communion, Book of Common Prayer)

This prayer, in its rather quaint Elizabethan English, reminds us that the Holy Spirit operates in many different ways. The different 'operations' of the Holy Spirit need to be distinguished, not confused.

There is an operation of the Holy Spirit in creation (Genesis 1:2). There is another operation of the Holy Spirit in creating life (Genesis 2:7). Therefore every human being who exists, who has been born into the world, owes his or her life and existence to the operation of the Holy Spirit in creation and in giving life.

We find later in the Bible that the Holy Spirit gives gifts of artistry and craftsmanship (Exodus 35:30–33), gifts of leadership (Judges 6:34; 1 Samuel 16:13), and gifts of prophecy (Isaiah 61:1). Such gifts are sometimes bestowed on surprising people, Samson for example, not so much according to the faith or holiness of the recipient, but according to the sovereign will of God. Peter Shaffer's play *Amadeus* (1980) is a meditation on the mystery of God's gift of music to Mozart, an apparently most unworthy recipient of God's extraordinary grace. Who can doubt that in 1940 the Spirit of God came on Winston Churchill to make him, in the words of A. J. P. Taylor, 'the saviour of his country'?[1]

The Holy Spirit is especially active in the events surrounding the birth of Jesus. Zechariah (Luke 1:67), Elizabeth (Luke 1:41), Simeon (Luke 2:25, 27) and John the Baptist himself (Luke 1:15) were all inspired prophetically by the Holy Spirit. Jesus 'by the operation of the Holy Ghost was made very man, of the substance of the Virgin Mary his mother'. But even though Jesus was from all eternity the Son of God and did not cease to be so at his birth in human form, at the River Jordan the Holy Spirit descended on him and remained on him in a new way.

The Holy Spirit operates on us in different ways as we come into that redemption which Jesus has won for us. His first work, when we are still in the world, is to convict us of sin, of righteousness and of judgement (John 16:8). Such conviction is the preliminary, or prevenient, work of the Spirit leading us to repentance and faith in Jesus as Lord and Saviour. It is the work of the Holy Spirit then to bring us to new birth (John 3:5). There is an analogy here to the operation of the Holy Ghost on the Virgin Mary, leading to the birth of Jesus. The Holy Spirit operates on us so that Jesus is born in us and we are born again in Christ.

Then there is a further work of the Holy Spirit in our lives, analogous to the Spirit's descent on Jesus at the River Jordan. This work of the Holy Spirit is called the 'baptism of the Holy Spirit' (John 1:33; Acts 1:5). I believe that both Scripture and present-day Christian experience demonstrate that this is a

1 A. J. P. Taylor, *English History 1914–1945* (OUP, 1965), p. 4 (footnote).

separate and distinct operation of the Holy Spirit from regeneration or new birth. The Scriptures provide a variety of examples of people who believed in Jesus and became disciples of
his who were only baptised with the Holy Spirit on some sub-
sequent occasion: Peter and the other apostles (Acts 2:1–4), the
Samaritans (Acts 8:14–17), Paul (Acts 9:17), and the Ephesians
(Acts 19:1–7). Many contemporary Christians also testify to
receiving Jesus and to receiving the baptism of the Holy Spirit
as two separate and distinct events in their spiritual lives. I am
one of these.

There are two sources of confusion in this discussion. First,
it is clear that in the apostolic church Christians who were not
baptised in the Holy Spirit were abnormal. The church universally expected that someone who repented and was baptised (in
water) in the name of Jesus for the forgiveness of their sins
would and should receive the gift of the Holy Spirit (Acts
2:38). The progression was not automatic, but the church took
care to ensure that in all cases it was completed. So Paul can
write with confidence to the Corinthians, 'We were all baptised
by one Spirit' (1 Corinthians 12:13). A plain reading of this
passage indicates that Paul is talking about the baptism of the
Holy Spirit, not baptism in water, and that the baptism of the
Holy Spirit is regarded as normal, not exceptional, in the early
church. What was exceptional in the early church was believers
who were not baptised in the Holy Spirit. That should not,
however, lead us to conclude that the same must automatically
be true in the church today. On the contrary, we face a situation in the church at large where the baptism of the Holy Spirit
is regarded as abnormal, and Christians who are baptised in
the Holy Spirit are regarded in many church circles as fanatics
or freaks. Thankfully the situation is slowly changing as more
and more new Christians are introduced to the baptism of the
Holy Spirit as a normal part of their Christian initiation.

A second source of confusion arises from the terminology
that we use. The Scriptures say of many people that they are
'filled with the Spirit'. The phrase is used of most of the people

we looked at earlier. The phrase 'filled with the Holy Spirit' is, however, nonspecific as to the particular way in which the Holy Spirit is operating. Bezalel, Gideon and John the Baptist are all 'filled with the Holy Spirit', but in very different ways and for very different purposes. The Holy Spirit comes on Simeon, Mary and Jesus, but again in different ways and for different purposes. In the life of the early church the phrase 'filled with the Spirit' invariably means baptised in the Holy Spirit, but it adds another dimension to this experience.

To speak of the baptism of the Holy Spirit, on the analogy of baptism in water, suggests a once-for-all event. And, indeed, there is in the life of every believer a first time when they are filled with the Holy Spirit. But the Scriptures also make it clear that being filled with the Holy Spirit is a continuing or continuous event in the life of the Christian. In Ephesians 5:18 Paul makes an implicit comparison between being filled with the Holy Spirit and getting drunk (he was not the first to do so – see Acts 2:13). The alcoholic needs to start drinking all over again every day in order to maintain his state of inebriation. Just so, Christians need to be filled with the Holy Spirit again every day in order to maintain their state of Spirit-filled grace.

Finally, I believe that such a theology of the baptism of the Spirit is supported by and illuminates the traditional sacramental practice of the church. The Catholic Church knows of two sacraments of initiation, baptism and confirmation. The sacramental sign of the first is water, and of the second the laying on of hands or anointing with oil. As the understanding and experience of baptism in the Holy Spirit was largely lost in the church during the Middle Ages, so the meaning and place of confirmation also became lost. A Church of England report on Christian initiation in 1971 opened with the words, 'The Church of England at the Reformation inherited the confusion of the Western Church over the significance of Confirmation.'[2]

---

2 *Christian Initiation* (General Synod of the Church of England, 1971), GS30, p. 9.

It continued by referring to confirmation as 'a rite in search of a convincing theological justification for its existence'. The fact that the church has retained this sacramental memory that there were once two stages to Christian initiation indicates that, corresponding to the two outward and visible signs, there were and should still be two inward and spiritual graces: regeneration by the Holy Spirit (water baptism) and being filled with the Holy Spirit (Spirit baptism) – two separate events. The Pentecostal and charismatic renewals are the recovery in the church of the reality to which this second sign points.

Shapes of the Church to Come

by Bishop Michael Nazir-Ali

As a leading Bishop in the Church of England, Michael Nazir-Ali could justly be called a pillar of the establishment. But this book is a clear demonstration that even the pillars realise that the building could collapse if radical changes are not implemented soon – changes that will involve a serious re-evaluation of the church's mission and ministry in today's world.

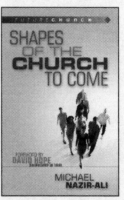

'This book provides thought-provoking insight on the most pressing issue facing the church today.'
Steve Chalke, Founding Director, Oasis Trust

'Bishop Michael Nazir-Ali explores some of the crucial questions facing the churches in the next decade...'
John Reardon, OBE
Former General Secretary of the Council of Churches for Britain and Ireland

'Rooted in Scripture and forged in pastoral practice, the key insights in this book address global and local issues that must not be ignored if the church is to stay alive and relevant.'
David Coffey, President, Baptist Union

FUTURE**CHURCH**

To Canterbury with Love

by Gavin Reid

Often amusing, sometimes moving and always affectionate, this is a picture of the contemporary Church of England unlike any other.

Gavin Reid has been in the middle of everything he describes, from Sunday School boy to member of the House of Bishops. Deftly he moves us from the fun of an East London parish in the sixties to the tension of a General Synod debate on homosexuality in the nineties; and much more.

A fascinating read for those inside the Church of England, this should also be required reading for those outside the Church who want to cut through media stereotypes and glimpse something of the reality.

Gavin Reid is President of British Youth for Christ. He was Bishop of Maidstone from 1992 to 2000 and received his OBE for his work in relation to the place of Christ in the millennium celebrations.